BOOK DESCRIPTION

You've been fed a lie. Losing weight is not just about food. It's connected to what makes you reach for something to eat when you feel overwhelmed, even though afterward, you feel more miserable than ever.

Losing Weight Is an Inside Job is for everyone trapped in a cycle of dieting and self-punishment. After decades of struggling, and having achieved lasting weight loss herself, Katy Landis presents powerful tools to help you lose weight for good. Changing her thinking ultimately allowed her to gain control over her eating. What worked for her can work for you too.

Discover the secret to feeling great about yourself while you lose weight and keep it off. Permanently. Learn to deal with painful experiences without being at the mercy of your emotions before taking the first bite. Forget obsessing over calories. Find out how one small change at a time will improve your mind, body, and life.

LOSING WEIGHT IS AN INSIDE JOB

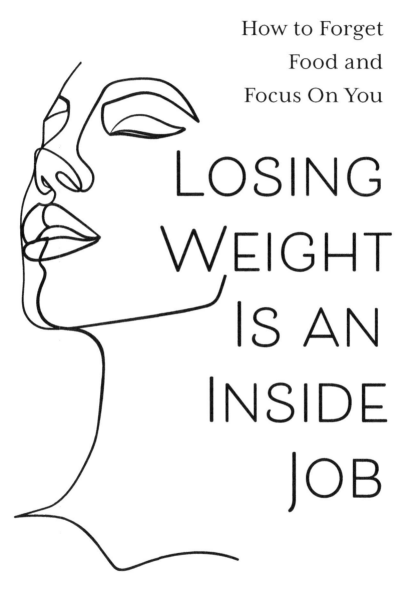

How to Forget
Food and
Focus On You

LOSING
WEIGHT
IS AN
INSIDE
JOB

Katy Landis

LIONCREST
PUBLISHING

LOSING WEIGHT IS AN INSIDE JOB

How to Forget Food and Focus On You

FIRST EDITION

ISBN   978-1-5445-3362-9 *Paperback*

978-1-5445-3361-2 *Ebook*

For those who always want more.

CONTENTS

INTRODUCTION

When I was pregnant for the second time, I gained about sixty pounds. I was forty years old then, and a lot of that extra weight wasn't a baby. I was hungry all the time, even though I constantly snacked on cheese sandwiches, cakes, and biscuits. There was no satisfying that hunger, though I certainly tried.

I had been trying my whole life.

With a toddler in tow and the new baby on the way, I kept about my daily tasks as best I could. This included regular trips to the shops, where I had become familiar with the staff, and we would pass a few pleasantries as I paid for my items. One day late in my pregnancy, I waddled in to pick up a few bits. When the shopkeeper looked up from her work, her eyes landed directly on my belly.

"Oh my, you're huge! Are you having a baby or an elephant?"

For just a moment, my vision blurred. She was smiling. It was a joke! Just some light humour at the shops.

Oh, how we both laughed together—but my insides were churning. The shopkeeper had taken my deepest shame and said it aloud. She made clear what I, of course, already knew.

I was fat.

Although I don't think she meant any malice, she also had no idea how she had hurt me. It was only when I got home behind the safety of my front door that I let the tears flow. The problem was not that I felt someone had been unkind to me. It was that I *hated* how big I had become.

I felt lost about how to change things, apart from another diet. But I already knew how that turned out.

The shopkeeper had no idea that her remark brought me to my lowest point that day. It's hard to maintain a smile when you are in pain.

And I had been hurting for a long, long time.

DESPERATION CAN FUEL US

It's so easy to blame ourselves for failing to lose weight. I should know. I struggled for decades to lose the weight and keep it off, but all I had to show for it was a solid track record of yo-yo dieting and a wardrobe that spanned eight sizes. I could do very well on a two-week diet, or even a six-week diet. I stuck to the plan, starving myself with whatever the fad was this time, and the pounds would disappear.

The moment the diet ended and I was left to my own devices, however, I just could not stop eating.

I didn't know how to live with food. I was either dieting or over-eating. There was no healthy middle ground.

For nearly my whole life, I could not stop eating. I tried to gain control by dieting, but that didn't help. Whenever I went on a diet, my body was starved of nutrients, so the hunger was real. Even though I was aware that I didn't have any control over my eating, even though I *knew* it was self-destructive behaviour, I simply could not stop.

And I wanted to stop, desperately. I wanted to be slim. I wanted to enjoy my time with other people instead of obsessing about the food. When could I eat? Do they know I hate how I look? Do they notice I've gained back the pounds?

I worked very hard to keep these thoughts to myself. I managed my facial expressions and made sure to keep up conversations and laugh at the jokes. I never missed a cue. I looked absolutely fine to the outside world, as though my extra weight was of no concern. I would show up to life as if I was okay.

I was not.

You may also be very good at putting up a front. We learn to hide, and soon it becomes second nature.

But it still hurts.

By the time I found myself in my forties, still overweight and sobbing over a shopkeeper's offhand remark, I knew something had to change. I was stretched to the limits in my personal life, with a growing family, a marriage that needed tending, and an ageing parent relying on me to solve her problems as well as mine. I was also obsessed with my weight and the food that dictated that number: *what* I ate, *when* I ate, *how much* I ate.

Ironically, my battle with food and eating opened the door that led to transformation. My desperation forced me to change my outlook on life. I could continue to fuel the downward spiral I was on, trying and failing again and again to find the diet that would solve my problems for good. But dieting was fueling the madness: I always ended up putting the weight back on, often even more than before.

Or I could choose a different way by looking at what was really going on. I discovered that the root cause of my overeating was in between my ears—it was in my mind. All this time, I had been looking in the wrong direction. I had been looking at the food, not at my thinking. When I changed my thinking, my body also changed. For good.

That was fifteen years ago. I lost over sixty pounds. I did this without going hungry, taking medications, or exercising every day. Instead, I accomplished the weight loss by healing and by addressing what was really going on *inside*.

And I discovered how to feel good again—how to love and care for myself so completely that I no longer need food to do it for me.

Now I have a different way to deal with painful situations and difficult emotions. I have tools based on nurturing, love, and understanding. And by using these tools, I can find a deep peace and healing that leads to a full life, not a full belly.

And this book will help you do the same.

LIFE STARTS TODAY—NOT TOMORROW

If you picked up this book looking for a way out of your weight struggles, I want to help you. You know you are carrying extra weight. You also know the pain of constant dieting, and that desperate hope that this time, somehow, it will be different. Past experience has shown you that the minute you come off the diet, however, the weight comes back, often leaving you bigger than before you went on the diet.

Every experience has shown that diets don't work, yet we keep coming back to them, hoping for a different outcome.

This book is not a diet plan. It's a life plan.

There's that nagging feeling that life—the *good* life—is going to begin sometime in the future. It's somewhere over there, just out of reach, that magical day when you're in a slim body. And should you actually reach that day, it doesn't last long, because the seduction of food and the obsessive need to keep eating wraps its arms around you and pulls you back in.

And who do you blame for all of this pain? Usually, yourself. You blame yourself because you think the problem has to do with your own lack of willpower. If only you tried hard enough, everything would be alright.

My friend, that is simply not true. You have been duped. Diets are not sustainable—yet we blame ourselves for something our willpower and our bodies cannot sustain. We want a quick fix, and instead, we are left with guilt, shame, and feelings of inadequacy.

Until now, no one has shown you that there is another way to be healthy.

And it has nothing to do with food.

A PROCESS, NOT AN EVENT

Food can numb, punish, and even comfort us, all at the same time. It can be your best friend or your worst enemy. There's no in-between. Moderation doesn't work for people like us. This idea that we should be able to open up a packet of biscuits, eat one, and put the rest away for later? I mean, who does that? Not me, that's for sure. On my best days, I might have been able to eat half the packet and stop, but then it would just call me back again and again, until it was all gone.

But why is the food calling you in the first place? That is what we will explore in this book. When you get to the *why*, you will finally be able to work through the *how* of better eating. But it turns out that the *why* almost never has anything to do with the food itself.

If the food is calling us and we are not actually hungry, what is really going on?

That is what this book is about. Together, we will explore the thoughts and emotions that drive your eating from the inside. We'll work to understand why we turn to food, and how we can heal ourselves from years of suffering to move forward into the life you deserve.

It's an inside job. This work will require a willingness to open up and be honest with yourself. It can be painful, but we will approach it carefully, in three steps: awareness, acceptance, and action.

First, we will become aware of all of the reasons you may eat—reasons that hide below the surface, deep in your mind. Once you learn to recognise why you approach food the way you do and understand what's really going on, you can work towards accepting yourself the way you are.

And with acceptance, you will finally be ready to act. It is only once we understand ourselves deeply and accept ourselves fully that we can make better choices. These actions, when they come from a place of healing rather than a temporary diet, will transform us.

Change is a process, not an event. It takes time, and it takes work. If you are in the never-ending cycle of pain—not wanting to overeat, but still hurting yourself with food and then hating yourself even more for your perceived weakness—you are in the right place. I can take you on this journey for one reason: I have been there myself, and I've come through the other side.

This is not a book based on just theory, but a transformation that has been felt, experienced, and lived. I spent decades searching for the quick-fix to my weight problem, my food problem, and it turns out that the quick-fix doesn't exist.

There is another way that doesn't involve calorie-counting, going hungry, or dieting. It does, however, require the courage to approach your life in a different way.

You want to lose weight and keep it off. By looking within to identify the root cause of what is really going on, what is really making you reach out for the food that you don't want to eat, you are making an active choice to live differently. Permit me to walk you through, step-by-step, until you have mastered everything necessary to get results.

The bottom line is that you will have to deal with *being yourself*—and that includes coexisting with uncomfortable feelings without turning to food. Instead, you will discover new tools, new coping skills, and new joys. You will stop berating yourself for all your past mistakes. After all, they have brought you to where you are today. They have brought you to this moment, and you are ready to change. You are ready to embrace the life you've been waiting for.

Turn the page—tomorrow is here.

PART ONE

AWARENESS, ACCEPTANCE, ACTION

You can't begin to change your life—much less your body—until you become fully aware of how your emotions cause you to act out in unhealthy ways. Losing weight is an inside job, so the work begins with understanding your mind and all the ways it tricks you into trying to numb your feelings with food. Becoming self-aware can be uncomfortable and even painful, but it is a journey that will lead you to full acceptance of who you are as a person.

This self-acceptance is something that most of us have been putting off, as we are so used to looking towards a future when we are finally slim. But ironically, it is only when we begin to accept who we are that the weight can begin to come off. Even though weight loss is your goal, it is actually the side effect of the larger healing. Once you embrace awareness and acceptance, you can finally take actions that will open the door to the life you've always wanted.

Let's begin.

CHAPTER 1

IT'S ALL IN THE MIND

I was on my knees, folded over in despair, surveying the carnage of wrappers, tins, and bags.

I had eaten the entire contents of the mini fridge in the hotel: crisps, chocolate bars, biscuits. It was all gone.

As I held the letter from my mother, I felt myself getting sucked back down into the downward spiral that had defined so much of my emotional life at that point.

"This time, I really mean it—I'm leaving him for good."

The letter had been waiting for me when I checked in. I was so excited to receive it! I had been travelling and had not been able to speak with my mother in over a month. It was the early 1990s, and I was in my twenties and working abroad. In the era before texting and instant messaging, she had to make a concerted effort to write me a letter, get it in the post, and wait at least a week for me to receive it.

Since my early teens, my mother had been turning to me to counsel her about her relationship with my stepfather. It was a revolving, downward spiral—the screaming breakups, the elation of reconciliations. I was always so relieved to hear her say she was leaving a relationship that brought her so much pain, then devastated when it never happened. I believed her every time, no matter how often she said it and didn't follow through. Each time, she would convince me that *this time* we'd make it to the other side and start a new life.

But we never did. We just spun round in circles, sucked further down the spiral.

As I read through the familiar words—she'd broken up with him, she was a heartbroken wreck, she'd been crying for days, she didn't know what to do—it was all too much for me. I opened the minibar, and didn't stop eating until I'd cleaned it out. The minibar had been full of crisps, chocolate, and biscuits—but now was empty.

As soon as the contents of the minibar were stuffed down, I was feeling even more wretched than before. Not only did I feel devastated for my mother, but now I'd done something to myself that made it even worse. The shame of it was crushing.

Okay, next week I won't eat much to balance out what I just did.

For the next five or six days, I ate only fruits. It was a familiar routine: overeating to feel safe, feeling like a failure about what I had just done, then going on a diet to make it all okay again.

I was always at the mercy of my feelings, but the cycle was the same: always spiralling, taking me down with it. Having a challenging day? Things not going as planned? Eat, rinse, repeat.

And yet, no one ever suspected. I was great at putting on a front.

WHAT'S REALLY GOING ON HERE?

How do you allow yourself to consume a minibar? Or a family-size bag of crisps? Or a tub of ice cream in one sitting?

This is eating as a means of escape. It works in the moment, and you forget all about the pain you're feeling as long as you're putting food in your mouth. Then because it's working, it's difficult to stop. If you're stuck in that downward spiral, you already know what happens when you *do* stop: the pain comes back and hits you tenfold, because not only are you stuck with the pain you were feeling before, but you have now added the devastation of what you've just done to yourself. The only way to keep all that pain at bay is to carry on eating. Except that eating doesn't really yield what we want, beyond the very fleeting seconds of comfort, numbing, and the mindlessness of it.

You want to have a slim body, eat less food, and eat healthy food, yet you can't stop the eating, even though doing it fills you with self-hatred. So you diet, you lose weight, you put it back on—and for most of us, we always put on that bit extra.

At that point in my life—let's just call it "the minibar incident"—I understood there was a connection between my feelings and my eating. I just didn't know what to do about it. The only way I could feel safe with food was to put myself on a diet.

Diets felt good because they provided boundaries. The diet told me what to do. Unfortunately, it wasn't sustainable. For three days, a whole week, maybe even two, I would feel safe—but the moment it finished, I just didn't know how to be in a world of food without being told what to eat. I didn't know how to coexist with food, much less do so in a healthy way.

Of course I knew how to undereat, too, but that didn't save me from my feelings. I was at the mercy of my own whims, whatever I needed in the moment. If I was in pain, I would dive into eating. When that got to be too much, I would go on a diet or pick at food, grazing all day to get a little bit of numbing with each bite.

I didn't know how to stop eating! I thought I was stuck with this body, and if I could just have a slim body instead, my life would be perfect.

Gaining weight is not just a physical problem. No diet I have tried—low-carb, cabbage soup, diet drinks, or intermittent fasting—has ever worked long-term. We have a 100 percent fail rate with diets, and yet we start again. I was good at dieting, and I could lose the weight. It was knowing what to do *after I finished the diet* that was the problem. I couldn't even enjoy the fact that I could fit into certain trousers again because I was lost to the world of food, and the slow, inevitable climb would begin again.

Many of us think losing weight is the answer, but then we lose some and discover we still feel the same. So we gain it back, because we haven't dealt with the root cause of our need to turn to food in the first place.

What drives us to reach out to food? We're not really dealing with the thinking that makes us overeat in the first place. **Aware-ness** is key; we must acknowledge the connection between our overeating and unresolved—or unidentified—feelings.

That doesn't make it easy, but it's your first step. And if you're any-thing like I was, you're desperate enough to emerge from the dark place that you're ready to try something completely different.

You can make a transformational change, and it begins with awareness.

In order to have a different relationship with food, we must also start thinking differently about ourselves. We've been doing this out of order, thinking we must achieve a weight or body that's worthy before we can deem ourselves valuable. But you are already worthy. Now it's time to embrace the tools you need to understand yourself so that you can begin to heal today.

Whether you are a grazer, a gorger, an overeater, or maybe a combination of all three, your relationship with food actually starts between your ears. When it comes to food, you must change your perspective if you want to achieve a different result.

IT'S NOT THE FOOD, IT'S THE OBSESSION

The root cause of overeating lies in your thinking—not in the food itself. It's an obsession.

We obsess about the food. When we feel anxious and low, we turn to the very thing that will destroy us and send us spiralling out of control. We wake up thinking about food, we think about it all day, and then it's the last thing we think about before we go to sleep at night. *How much should I eat? Will I be able to stop when*

I start eating that? Or would it be better to have that and not this? The constant body comparison and thinking about what life will be like when we're slim are also part of that line of thinking.

If we accept this about ourselves—that we really can be obsessed with food—we open the door to a whole new way of looking at weight loss and at ourselves. And if it starts with obsession, then it's also fair to say that *the mind is where the obsessions start.*

For me, it started in my teens, after years of forming thought patterns that had time to root and flourish. I was only a bit plump, but I was knowledgeable about calories and had it in my head that my caloric intake could not exceed 1,000 calories per day. It was like my brain had a barcode scanner that would constantly compute calories all day long. I would think about the combinations of foods that would add up to it, how to mix and match, strategise how to "beat" my own system by eating a lot of low-calorie foods, and so on. Eating wasn't a pleasurable experience because I was constantly monitoring everything that I ate. For the first four decades of my life—with the exception of early childhood—I can't remember a time when food was just food and not something to be battled with.

Sometimes it feels like our mind doesn't even belong to us, let alone the hands that reach out for something to pop into our mouths even when we've told ourselves we won't. It's a miserable existence. You can tell yourself it will be different this time. *I'll just have a few crisps or one biscuit,* you think. I know. I made the same promise, and then would carry on until the bag was empty. More self-hatred arrived with every crunch, crunch, crunch.

We are so used to blaming ourselves that we are not even aware of the extent of our food obsession, how intertwined it is with our every thought. You want to lose weight more than anything else—it's constantly there, just out of reach, if only, if only, if only... We want it so badly, some of us are willing to jeopardise our health.

Because we are obsessed, our behaviour turns compulsive. The compulsion to eat has us eating things we didn't want or being unable to stop once we start. Now we feel worse, so we have another compulsion to eat, to make ourselves feel better.

So we travel further down the spiral.

When you have the awareness that the problem lies in your thinking, you have a completely different perspective. When you can change your thoughts, your body will follow. Food isn't the solution, and it will never be enough. It will only stop the pain momentarily.

It's *you* that has to be enough.

ANY OF THIS SOUND FAMILIAR?

Obsession starts in the mind, and when you live in your head, you are not fully present. There is a vicious, cyclical dialogue taking place where you blame yourself, but still pacify yourself with food:

You: "I feel so bloated and uncomfortable."

Also You: "Well, it's your own stupid fault. You shouldn't have eaten that yesterday."

You: "I'll just finish off those biscuits now and be good in the morning."

And the same dialogue rewinds, ready to run again tomorrow. It's always tomorrow.

So many of my clients have said that they always felt like they were waiting for their life to begin, thinking:

- *I can get that job...*
- *I can get that boyfriend...*
- *I can be who I really need to be...once I've lost weight.*

What about you? Do you have a running inner dialogue with yourself? Do you have a closet full of clothes that no longer fit, but you can't bear to give up on them? Do you feel like a failure, regardless of how successful you are in other aspects of your life?

These are the questions and thought patterns that arise from your obsession with food.

QUIZ: ARE YOU OBSESSED WITH FOOD?

Answer the following questions honestly with a simple *yes* or *no*:

- Do you eat when you're not hungry?
- Do you struggle to stop eating even when you want to?
- Have you tried many diets and weight loss plans only to put the weight back on?
- Do you turn to food when you are upset or bored?
- Do you constantly think about food or how much you weigh?

- Do you ever eat lots of food in one sitting or graze all day?
- Do you feel desperate, hopeless, and ashamed about your weight?
- Do you sometimes eat alone so nobody will see the amount or what food you are eating?
- Do you feel life would be great if only you were slim?
- Do you blame yourself for what you think is your lack of self-discipline?
- Do you often feel guilty about the food you eat?
- Do you constantly calculate the calories you have eaten?
- Do you feel good when on a diet and bad when eating?

If you answered *yes* to any of these questions, you are using something *outside* yourself to feel good about what's going on *inside* yourself. Obsession takes over our bodies, our minds, our emotions, our spirits, and our ability to connect with others in a healthy way.

Awareness is a key first step in healing from it.

IT'S NOT YOUR FAULT

Obsession is a strong word, and it's okay for it to bring up strong feelings when you apply it to your relationship with food. We often blame ourselves for it, thinking this is all about a lack of willpower.

At one point, I found a six-week diet and I thought, *Brilliant—six weeks. That will give me plenty of time to get this sorted.* And because I was quite young, I lost a lot of weight. The weight was coming off—as it would on any diet in which the first ten days consisted of eating only fruit—but I wasn't living life. When you're in your twenties, hungry and miserable, it isn't a great place to be. But that's where I'd landed on my six-week adventure, thinking my life would begin when the diet was finished.

Instead of my life beginning, I just went back to eating like crazy. I didn't learn anything, and that made me panic. My body was starved for nutrients after being on the diet, which added to my insatiable appetite. So I went for another six weeks, resigned to wondering if I'd be on the six-week diet for the rest of my life, destined to always be desperate and miserable. I would have to sit on the sidelines and be a spectator to everyone else having fun.

After twelve weeks of the six-week diet, I had the body I'd always wanted, but it only lasted a few days. I also knew deep down that the second I stopped, the numbers on the scale would eventually climb back up until I found the willpower to do it all over again.

And again.

And *again*.

This was my cycle for twenty-five years—each time, the downward spiral would suck me back in, taking me deeper into its cavity. It never produced a different outcome, but I was obsessed with trying to make it work.

If you're like me, you've tried dozens of quick-fix diets, yet you keep getting fatter. You are no longer dealing with just seven pounds to ten pounds. Now, you have a stone or two to lose, or more. You no longer recognise your own body.

The truth is *you are not a failure*. These diets are not designed to work long-term. They don't change your thinking; they don't get to the root causes of why you reach for the food in the first place. In the United States, more than 160 million people are on a diet at any given time.[1] If diets worked, surely we would all be slim. And we live in a world that surrounds us with these mixed messages—the supermarket that smells of sweet bread, the crisps being marketed in a very clever way, the super flavours added to hijack our taste buds, and the social media that leads us to compare and judge ourselves.

The obsession gets baked right in.

FEEL THE FEELINGS

There are four general ways we use food: to escape, to numb, to punish, to control. We'll dig into these later in the book, but for now, it's important to understand them as you work through the awareness of your food obsession. Once you know that you are doing this, it doesn't mean it will stop. It does, however, require you to acknowledge that you've been searching for something outside of yourself instead of going inward, where the real solutions can be found.

When we use food to **escape**, we don't want to be in our current reality. The fantasy world inside our heads is much nicer, and food gives us a quick rush—but it's a rush that never sustains us.

When we use food to **numb**, we're pushing down our uncomfortable feelings on a given matter. We don't want to feel the pain. We feel overwhelmed. We eat quickly to numb in the moment, without any thought of the consequences.

When we use food to **punish**, we don't believe we are worthy

---

[1]   "Diet & Weight Loss," Harvard Health Publishing, Harvard Medical School, accessed August 22, 2022, https://www.health.harvard.edu/topics/diet-and-weight-loss.

of better treatment. We may not have been treated well in the past, so we carry on the abuse by using food to punish ourselves.

When we use food to **control**, it's a paradox, because we have actually lost control. You need to control *something* in your life— in this case, what you put in your mouth in the moment—yet you're out of control when it comes to your relationship with that food. There's a loss of control when you overeat, but you are in control because you're the one eating, and it's a vicious paradox.

It's time to allow yourself to feel these feelings. You may not be able to identify all of the emotions just yet, so let's keep it simple. Think about the four ways you may be using food when you overeat: to escape, to numb, to punish, to control. Is there one that resonates with you more than the others?

Once you've reflected on the ways *you* use food in your life, it's time to acknowledge what you've been doing. Read the statements below and decide which ones apply to you.

- *I can't stop myself from eating and I don't know how to stop myself.*
- *I eat even when I'm aware that I'm not hungry.*
- *I turn to food when I'm upset, angry, deflated, or feeling low.*
- *I eat food to feel better, even though I know it's going to be momentary and I am going to feel worse afterward.*

Now, say the ones that describe you out loud or write them in a journal. Acknowledging that these statements are true about you is a courageous step. You're building the awareness that you use food to run away from yourself. This acknowledgement is a difficult thing to do, but also a brave thing to do.

YOUR NEW LIFE BEGINS HERE

The root cause of overeating lies in your thinking, not in the food itself. We eat to numb pain from various problems, and it can never work. Unless you have that awareness, you are just going to carry on doing the same thing that I did for decades: looking outside of yourself for the solution, instead of looking inside.

Yet *inside is where the power is*. This is where freedom lies.

So starting right now: no more diets, eating plans, or fasting. No more pain caused by the constant hope that *this time, it will be different*.

All this time, you thought it was your lack of willpower, not trying hard enough. But the truth is that you cannot fill the void with food. There is another way to be healthy and at peace, and it has nothing to do with food. It is, truly, all in your mind.

Thinking back to the minibar incident, I knew I had a problem. The diets were just an illusion of control. I would think, *I just need one more go*, and it would always start tomorrow. Morning would roll around, I would be on this strange high, thinking I was on the right track, drinking all the shakes or not eating for half the day. Eventually, when the diet was done, I'd end up spiralling because something happened at work or in my personal life that was hurtful or unfair. I wouldn't admit how those things made me *feel*, nor did I take a pause to consider what was true. I would just hit the refrigerator like a madwoman to numb the pain in the moment, without any thought of consequences.

Today, I can sit down and enjoy a delicious plate of food. I can love food now, and I know that when I finish, I'm satisfied. And I don't need to eat anything else.

Peace is available for you, too, and it can begin right now. You have the power to break free from these obsessions. You're here to try something different. It won't always be easy, but it is the real solution. What if you could rid yourself of old patterns and behaviours that aren't serving you or your health? I mean, banish them from your life forever? As we deal with each one, letting them wash over us, we'll examine what it is we really want—and actually take action to do something about it.

The extra weight is a physical manifestation of our inner turmoil. Your body isn't separate from your mind and your emotions. We have to address all three if we want to change our weight, our health, and our lives. With a new understanding of the importance of self-awareness on your weight loss journey, it's time to dig deeper into the inner workings of your thoughts and emotions to understand the mechanisms that play into your overeating.

CHAPTER 2

THE FEAR-EAT-REGRET CYCLE

If you weren't old enough to fall in love with the television show *Friends* during its original run, you've probably grown to love it in reruns. I loved all of the characters: these beautiful people with their very slim bodies who, when they go through a break-up, reach for a tub of ice cream that's almost as big as their heads. The cliché is *almost* funny, but it doesn't quite work in real life. Maybe you have also tried "ice cream therapy," thinking it will help you feel better—or at least, keep the pain away.

But at the end of the day, you don't end up looking like Jennifer Aniston.

Maybe ice cream isn't your go-to for solving your problems. Perhaps it's cakes, crisps, or some other food that gives you momentary relief from the emotional pain. Unlike the image of that tear-soaked ice cream therapy session on television, your eating isn't even pleasurable, because you know what is waiting for you on the other side. When you've finished crunching, you're left with a whole load of humiliation and guilt.

Every time you eat food in response to whatever is happening, the pain on the other side of it is all-consuming. That sends you back to the food, because you don't want to deal with what you are feeling, and this terrible cycle of pain continues. We don't see the psychological breakdown on "Friends" because it isn't funny or beautiful—but if you live this year after year, it is your reality.

It doesn't have to be.

UNDERSTANDING THE FEAR-EAT-REGRET CYCLE

In the previous chapter, we talked about the importance of **awareness**. You have hopefully completed the quiz and given thought to the ways your eating is tied to your emotional life. Now that you are more aware of your relationship with food, you need to acknowledge its presence and *directly address it by name*.

So let's name it: the **fear-eat-regret cycle**.

Feelings are not bad, but many of us do not have the tools to manage them. That doesn't mean we don't have them, experience them, and find another way to act out on them.

When we experience fear, we seek coping mechanisms in an attempt to control the chaotic world around us. In our fear, we often turn to food to numb the fear and emotions until they pass. When we finally stop eating, we feel deep regret for what we have just done. Since regret is another difficult emotion, new fears are triggered, and the cycle continues.

The fear-eat-regret cycle is vicious.

The triggers that set you off onto this cycle can be big pressures or small worries. They can even be caused by good news, like a new job or first date—things that are pleasurable but still elicit fear of the unknown.

Fears and anxieties are often related to unmet needs: when someone treats you badly, doesn't give you the respect you deserve, or makes you worry that they don't like you. These incidents don't have to have just happened to trigger your eating, either. Sometimes just remembering a painful moment can trigger the same fight or flight response that lands you right back at the refrigerator. In fact, the trigger doesn't even have to be real. It may just be your *perception* that somebody doesn't like you or that you don't fit in that sends you deeper into the fear-eat-regret cycle.

I mentioned earlier in the book that it helps to determine what we are *really* hungry for, but sometimes the questions are uncomfortable to sit with: *Why do I suddenly want that doughnut? Is it because I'm hungry, or is it because I'm not feeling listened to, heard, loved, or cherished? Am I feeling abandoned?* When we pause long enough to consider what is *really* going on, we stand a better chance of identifying our real need versus the impulsive, immediate gratification that puts us back in the fear-eat-regret cycle.

Let's look at each part of the fear-eat-regret cycle in greater detail to recognise how it manifests and how to stop it.

FEAR LIVES IN THE BODY

Fear is not comfortable, but it also isn't permanent. Feelings are not facts, but they can feel like a bullet to the heart. In order to manage them properly, it's important to grasp what's taking place in your body when they arrive.

Fear is an acute feeling, that initial fight-or-flight physical reaction you have when something goes wrong. There are sudden, huge fears that lead to a rush of adrenaline, but there are also underlying, lingering fears that result in a chronic, mid-level pain that's always with you.

When something terrible happens, you might feel a heaviness in the chest. The feeling is sudden and swift. The underlying fears, however, may produce a gnawing in the abdomen. You may have moments of happiness, but you're not feeling light and joyful. There's always a heaviness that lingers, and you hold it in your body.

The longer you hold on to these feelings, the more desperate you become for relief. Your lingering fears—whether of an actual event or of your unpleasant emotions—leads you to eat.

When your body is under stress, your adrenal glands release a range of hormones, including cortisol. Cortisol is also known as the stress hormone, and when it spikes in your bloodstream, it increases your breathing rate, blood circulation, and heart rate. This system is genetically designed and helped us survive in ancient times, providing our bodies the extra boost needed to escape a predator.

Even in modern times, the fight or flight response is extremely effective in helping you act quickly in the face of real danger. Unfortunately, it's not helpful for your tummy. When the stress response is triggered repeatedly by things like looming deadlines and family arguments, cortisol also increases the buildup of belly fat. This is why many people can't lose weight in problem areas like the stomach. Without realising it, they are constantly in survival mode, and their bodies are triggered to hold on to the weight as protection from a perceived threat.

Fear, then, leads to a one-two punch of pain: on an emotional level, you're desperate to do anything to escape the feeling. On a physical level, your body is programmed to respond to stress by holding on to fat, not releasing it.

No wonder we turn to food.

PEELING OFF THE LAYERS OF FEAR

When we're upset about something specific, like a missed promotion or a relationship that didn't work out, we might not realise that our fear is actually about something much deeper, such as not being heard or noticed. Whittling it down to the real issue takes time, so be gentle with yourself as you do this work.

If you're feeling upset or angry, it may only take a bit of pressure from the outside world for it to come out. The expression on someone's face could have you thinking, *they don't like me, they aren't listening, they are irritated with me,* and so on. Even someone stealing your parking space can set you off into this spiral of not feeling cared about.

Deep fears—the kind we don't want to stop and think about—often surface in small, external irritations. Start building a bridge between those everyday irritations and the much larger feeling underneath them. As always, the key question is, *What's really going on here?*

EATING AS A REACTION

When you don't want to deal with the discomfort of your triggered emotions, you slide right into the second part of the cycle:

You eat.

This eating might be manic and intense, or it might be calm and steady. But you cannot stop. You may eat until your body is physically uncomfortable. When you do this, you are transforming your emotional discomfort into physical discomfort, which is often easier to cope with. But of course, this doesn't address the real problem at all. You think you're trading one pain for the other when, in fact, you are exacerbating both—all because you're stuck in the cycle of fear-eat-regret.

Unfortunately, eating can become a deeply ingrained reaction to the stresses of life. It should be a pleasurable activity, but when eating is triggered by fear, we are not enjoying the food. When you rely on eating to numb your feelings and solve your problems, it eventually becomes a reflex—a knee-jerk reaction to every bump on the road of life.

When eating in reaction to pain becomes a habit, it's a completely mindless activity. We eat furiously, desperate to take our minds off of whatever's gone wrong around us. Because we actively seek to escape, we are not mindfully present to notice the delicious aroma, texture, and taste of our food.

When you eat to numb, you don't just push away the pain. You also push away the pleasure. It's a lose-lose situation.

And that loss—the utter inability to enjoy eating, despite feeling compelled to do more and more of it—leads directly to an over-whelming sense of regret.

REGRET: THE END AND BEGINNING OF THE CYCLE

Have you ever said or done something you wished you hadn't? For example, opening a box of biscuits and eating beyond one or two? We all know that feeling of regret, and we've all felt it many times.

Whether it's something you've said or something you've eaten, regret arrives to make you feel unworthy of anything but blame. It's almost like a madness that takes over, because you already know that when you turn to food, you're going to feel worse. You know that food isn't the solution, yet it's what you turn to as a solution every single time.

When I was eight years old, I was at a friend's house and noticed a big bowl of nuts and raisins had been put out for guests. I can remember eating them and not being able to stop. I felt uncomfortable about it, thinking, *Oh no, I've been bad. I will be good tomorrow.* Since I was only a child, I really didn't understand what was going on inside of me. In my eight-year-old mind, my parents had just got divorced, and that big bowl of food was just calling me.

So I ate.

And down the spiral I went. I felt bad and wrong inside, yet I didn't stop. I kept right on going, until I could eat no more and I was overwhelmed with regret.

Why do we binge? Why do we graze? Why do we expect different outcomes? Why do we have those "sod it" moments where we give up and give in?

We do it to make ourselves feel better. It's not about logic, but about need. The thing about regret is that it reminds us that we've done something wrong and triggers yet another fear: that deep down, we are bad. We are unworthy.

And this powerful fear drives us to eat again, pushing us off into another round of the fear-eat-regret cycle.

In my own adventures in dieting, I tried and failed over and over again. Every time, I ended up failing at some point, which only led me to gain even more weight and feel even worse about myself. In the process, I finally learned that, for me, there is no such thing as taking just one bite. One handful. One piece. No matter how often I told myself that's all I would have, deep down I knew that wasn't true. The concept of "just one" didn't exist for someone like me. So I would heap on more guilt, like a cherry on top.

Food is not the enemy, but it sure feels like it.

WHAT IS IT WITH ME?

I've had clients tell me how much they hate themselves for falling into the fear-eat-regret cycle. *I hate myself. I do this every time, no matter how many times I pledge to do tomorrow differently.* They feel like they are on the sidelines of their own lives, living in the shadows, and the bigger they get, the more self-conscious they feel about it all.

It's confusing. Many of them are successful professionals and have forged positive relationships. Their thought process is, *Why is my life together in all the major areas except this one? Why can't I get my act together here? Why does it hold such power over me?*

When it comes to eating, it's hard to admit to themselves that they are powerless.

To add to their confusion, we all have a primal need to eat. The human body requires food. We diet, then realise we're not getting enough energy. Now you're not only at the mercy of your emotions; you're also at the mercy of your biological need to eat because you've been undereating.

The only way out is through. You *can* free yourself from this obsession and regret.

We can get there with awareness and acceptance of what we're feeling and what we're needing. There is a spectrum of emotions, and when we try to numb the ones we don't want to feel, we actually deny ourselves the happiness and joy we could experience. By repressing the bad feelings, we also bury the good feelings.

THE FIRST STEP

When you are eating on emotion, you eat past the point where you feel physically comfortable. You're just chasing an illusion, rather than dealing with your feelings of shame and regret. At that stage, you're blaming yourself, you're angry with yourself, and you're thinking you are not good enough.

How do you *want* to feel after eating? It's time to create new behaviours and a new way of living so that your emotions don't have to rule you. The goal is to arrive at the point where you have a clear head and you're not being driven to eat everything within reach all of the time.

EXERCISE 1: OWN IT

Before you can create new results in your life, you must be able to see clearly the old patterns you've been living with.

Get a pen and paper and write down your answers to the following questions. Don't worry about getting anything "right." Just start writing and see what comes to you.

1. **What situations make you want to overeat?** Is it when you're tired or alone? Are these feelings tied to a particular time of day? Is it triggered by work or seeing certain people in your life? Or is the desire to overeat with you all of the time?
2. **Where does your overeating usually take place?** Is it behind closed doors? Is it when eating out with friends? Alone in your car?
3. **What time of day do you tend to overeat?** What's going on with you at this time? Are you more tired, more overwhelmed, or more irritable?

There are no right or wrong answers here, and it's okay if you change your mind or add something later. These answers are just for you.

Seeing your thoughts in black and white will help you to accept and then take responsibility for your behaviour. Read over your writing, and decide: are you ready to accept responsibility for this? If so, write that down too.

I take responsibility for this behaviour.

When we learn from our past, we can let go of regret and guilt. We can build a better future by learning to respond in a different way. To be human is to make mistakes. We can waste our time wishing things might have been different, but with new awareness, we have new choices.

EXERCISE 2: ADMIT IT

Next, we'll move towards practical application. Write down feelings and consequences before you eat. The first thought *before* you eat, not at the first bite. Get aware of the thought *before* you open the fridge and try to eat while in survival mode. Explain the feeling, write down how you will feel after, remind yourself that it needs to change:

What I'm actually feeling is ____. What I actually need is ____.

Remember, we are peeling back layers, so keep asking yourself, *What's really going on here?*

Start with the everyday irritations, but probe until you reach the much larger, underlying feeling. For example, your knee-jerk reactions to situations might sound like this:

Amy got the credit for my work.

John didn't call.

I don't want to go. I know they won't like me.

Instead of thinking Amy and John are the problem, use these thoughts to swing open the door and reveal the root feeling that's been hiding underneath all the others. That's the feeling that has been eating away at your *self*, and no matter how much food you consume, you can't fill the gaping hole it has left.

Your behaviour won't change overnight, but it is the beginning of awareness and moving to a place where you can start to see patterns. This second exercise has to be done *in the moment* as we're moving from theory to practical life skills. Each time you finish the sentence above, wait five minutes—let's call it the "five-minute pause"—before you decide whether you are truly hungry. Set a timer or use the clock on your mobile phone to hold yourself accountable as you pause to explore your true feelings.

Be kind to yourself during this process, because you won't always get to your brain on time to take that pause. Keep at it until you do. Remember, this is about our thoughts and feelings. There's a moment when you think about eating, know it will happen, and the mere *thought* of food momentarily numbs the feeling. That's when to step in!

THE POWER OF THE PAUSE

Why do I want you to stop while the anticipation of eating is still in your head? Whenever you reach for food, there's a split second of decision—the moment when you know it's going to happen. You're going to eat. You haven't actually opened the package, but there's the *thought* that you're going to do it, to momentarily numb the feeling that's trying to reveal itself. That moment is so brief, it's practically knee-jerk—we're not aware that we can actually control it.

I'm not talking about the moment before you take that first bite, or even the moment that you reach for the food—by then, it's too late. I'm talking about the exact moment the *thought* of eating pops into your head, before you put yourself in fast-forward and eat whatever you can get your hands on.

As you practice the Own It and Admit It exercises, you'll learn the timing of thought-to-mouth and pinpoint the moment—of self-punishment, numbing, self-soothing, or a combination—that occurs before you reach to take that first bite. Think about slowing down to pinpoint what each moment feels like—*What is your body doing? What emotion prompted the thought of eating? How often does this feeling prompt this behaviour?*—so you can build new reflexes that *respond* instead of react.

ACCOUNTABILITY WITHOUT JUDGEMENT

When you're dieting, you feel like you're on the right track—right up until something triggers your emotions and the diet goes out the window. Or you might be very good at sticking to a diet for a certain time, but the moment it finishes and the boundaries are gone, you fall right back into the cycle. You don't know how to process what just happened, so you call yourself a failure.

Here is a truth to tell yourself: *It's not your fault.*

This is literally the way you have been using food to cope with life. You cannot blame yourself for that because it gets ingrained inside us at quite a young age. This is how we cope with things we don't understand. On top of that, the billion-pound processed food industry has hijacked your taste buds with food containing additives and strong flavours that leave you wanting more. This sort of food is everywhere, and you're at its mercy *by design.*

As you get better at the five-minute pause, look out for any patterns you may notice. What happened just before "the thought" entered your mind? Where were you? Which emotions blasted through? What was your body's physical reaction?

When I work with clients, I always ask them to fill out a food diary for three days each week—two days during the week and one day during the weekend—and to record every bite of food they eat. When listing foods, it's important to include portion size too, as even a teaspoon of peanut butter will eventually add up.

I also ask them to tell me how they *felt* at the time. To do this, they rate their hunger and describe what they were feeling, both before and after eating. They don't have to write much. It could be simply "I feel fine" or "upset" and move on. The point is to try and get a picture of how food rules their lives and governs their emotions on a daily basis.

You can use the same food diary for each meal of the day.

DAILY FOOD DIARY

TIME	FOOD	EMOTIONS BEFORE EATING	EMOTIONS AFTER EATING

Whether you use the full template above or just write your thoughts as a note on your mobile, the idea is to gain awareness and hold yourself accountable—*without* judgement. Even clients who report that they eat healthy foods are usually shocked to discover how much they consume, once they keep track of every bit of snacking and grazing. Many are eating more in between the meals than they are during the actual meals. A complete understanding of your eating habits and thought patterns is key.

You will never change until you take notice and get off the hamster wheel. Awareness helps to break the cycle; it's the catalyst to help you find another way to be healthy—a true way that integrates the health of your mind, body, and spirit.

THE GOOD PART OF REGRET

Going back to those familiar scenes on *Friends*, what happens when Rachel or Chandler grabs the ice cream to cope with a breakup? Another friend would find them and stay with them until the moment passed. One of the reasons the show was such a hit is because it was all about connection: they laughed together, cried together, and cared for one another.

There is no shortcut through the pains and problems that come with life; we simply have to work our way through them. The fear-eat-regret cycle is devastating. It leads to some really destructive behaviour. But—if you're willing—regret can be channelled as part of the solution. If you didn't have the regret, you would never change what you were doing.

How can we use regret as the springboard to a new beginning?

That pain that you feel—the regret you feel—can pave the way. It's not easy to turn over a new leaf, and when everything is kind of okayish, you won't do it. But when you really *do* hit that pain, stop. Turn around. It's an opportunity to open a door.

Haven't you had enough?

Once you recognise how you use food all the time, one of the most beautiful things you can do is figure out how to handle things in a different way. That doesn't mean it will all be different from that point on—it might be three steps forward, two steps back—but once you've tried a different approach, and you know that you *can* do it, you're more likely to try that way again. Be kind to yourself as you move towards this new path.

Identifying the source of your pain and fear is the first baby step to break the cycle. Once you call it by name—acknowledge and accept its presence—it can no longer overstay its welcome. But every time you break the cycle by acknowledging and proactively exploring your fear, you are being true to yourself. This is how you break the cycle that has had control over you for far too long.

It's all about changing our perspective. When overwhelming emotions hit us, we *can* learn to think with a clear mind before taking that first destructive bite. By developing a deeper awareness of how your mind operates in relation to food, you can move towards clarity and acceptance.

CHAPTER 3

EXPECTATIONS AND ACCEPTANCE

"No matter how often I ask, Tom forgets to take out the rubbish."

I was listening to Jen, a client, give me examples of why she was unhappy with her husband and her marriage. The rubbish, especially, drove her mad.

"We always end up in a huge argument every weekend," she continued. "It seems to me that if he really cared about me, he would just take the bins out. It's such a small thing, but it would mean so much. Why is that too much to ask?"

The rubbish bin wasn't picked up until the weekend, but Jen was already fixated on it by midweek. Her obsession gave birth to new irritations, which put her in a constant state of turmoil with Tom. By this point, she had amassed a collection of wrong-doings—past, present, and perceived—all the while ignoring the actual source of her irritations.

Moaning at Tom produced the opposite of the intended effect. My sense was that he resisted this particular chore because he was feeling controlled. The more she railed against him, the more he was sticking his heels in about it because he didn't like to be told what to do. It was a vicious cycle, to the point where it no longer even mattered who was right or who was wrong. Jen could not let it go. It was symbolic, in her mind, of how little Tom cared about her.

The more that they argued about it, the more expectations Jen would build up around the issue: Surely he would take out the bins just to stop the argument. Surely he could take five minutes to do that because he can see it's causing me so much pain and upset. And surely if he loved me, he would just do this for me! It was such a small thing, but she would obsess about it for days—was he going to take it out? Would he care enough about her? To her, this is what taking out the rubbish came down to—if Tom cared, he would look after her, do her wishes, and meet her expectations.

In her moments of obsession, Jen would graze. Midweek, it would start as low-level anxiety—a handful of jelly beans, a few spoonfuls of jam—but as the week progressed, so did her eating. Leftover pudding from last night's dinner, a tablespoon of peanut butter—Jen would eat whatever she could find. Tom was startled by how worked up she got, and Jen would feel disappointed with herself, angry with Tom, and just wanted the food to numb it all.

We've seen this cycle before.

Because you and I are not emotionally involved in her story, we can see that Jen was making a big deal out of something very small. But it was not small to Jen. Deep down, it wasn't about a simple chore. It was about her feeling cared for and secure that her husband was tuned into her feelings.

What Jen didn't see, however, was that her *expectations* were causing all her pain.

History had shown her that rubbish collection was not something Tom prioritised, but Jen continued to rail against it. Like swatting at flies, it's the small things that get to us—they distract from the deeper issues that we are trying to ignore. Had Tom snapped to attention, Jen likely would have found some other small thing to rant about and insist that it meant Tom didn't care enough.

But Tom *did* care, and had other ways he showed it. So how could Jen move past her obsession?

The answer lies in setting realistic expectations and accepting the world and the people around us as they are—not as we wish them to be.

WHY IS ACCEPTANCE IMPORTANT?

Our expectations about the world can often be unrealistic. When reality doesn't align with our expectations, it makes us unhappy. It's human nature to want to be loved and respected. We crave that feeling, so it's easy to pin our emotion on the simple act of someone taking out the bins, meeting us somewhere on time, or remembering our anniversary.

The thought process goes like this: *If he loved and cared for me, he would do* _____. It all seems small, so you don't even recognise the whole drama going on deeper in your psyche. It's an expectation that isn't met, and how that plays out results in a number of irritations—or in Jen's case, a standing weekly argument.

Disappointment can hit us hard. When people don't behave in the way we wish they would, or when things don't go the way we had planned, we can feel let down. Then we internalise this sadness and somehow come to believe that it is our fault. We must not be good enough, or loved enough, or worthy of happiness. The suffering can become unbearable and send us directly to food to fill the void.

The opportunity for growth and change comes from accepting that we only have control over ourselves. Our unhappiness comes from unrealistic or unmet expectations of others. When you can accept the reality of other people's behaviour, you have the key that allows you to let go of the past and move into the present and future.

Acceptance isn't defeat; it's actually a form of empowerment. You can't change other people, much less their emotions and behaviours, but with acceptance, you can change yourself and your perspective. *Acceptance is not submission.* It's just acknowledging reality as it is today, right now. It doesn't mean you can't make decisions or take action to change things.

Our expectations cause us so much frustration and keep us feeling like a victim. We understandably want other people to behave in a way that will make us happy. But then we are continually disappointed when someone or some situation fails to meet our expectations.

This disappointment comes even when someone has let us down again and again. Remember the minibar incident? My mother was always telling me she was leaving my stepfather to start a new life. Looking back, this happened three or four times a year, and I believed her every time. No matter how many times she'd promised me, although she would completely mean it when she would say it, history showed me a 100 percent track record that it would never happen. My expectations were not based in reality.

So I carried on, always wanting to pin my peace on somebody else's behaviour, whether it was my mother, a friend, or a boyfriend. There was a constant void waiting to be filled, and I knew just how to fill it: with food. It was a pattern that I would continue to live out, looking for the solution in all the wrong places.

There is nothing wrong with having high standards, but we must also be prepared to accept reality if results fall short of our expectations. Otherwise, we risk our disappointment manifesting in unhealthy ways, including stuffing ourselves with food.

THE PARADOX OF POWER

When we talk about regaining and holding on to our power, we must be willing to relinquish the desire to control. That seems contradictory, doesn't it? Especially when our eating is so out of control! When we hold on to our expectations for dear life, we give our power away. We have to reconnect to ourselves, step out of this inner dialogue, and move forward in gratitude.

We put our value in someone else's hands, and when they don't behave in a way that we want, or a situation doesn't turn out the way we had hoped, we think our value has diminished. Because we're so emotionally involved, we take things personally. We can't live in their heads or fully understand their motives, so we assume the problem is us.

When you get stuck in these patterns of expectation, disappointment, and feeling victimised, you remain trapped in thoughts like:

- *If I could just control this...*
- *If I could just get someone to...*
- *If only they would...*
- *If I had just...*

And while your thoughts spiral, you give away your power to that person or situation, thinking you can't be happy unless everything measures up to your expectations.

You can stop putting your feelings of peace, safety, and joy in other people's hands—that is an inside job that cannot be handled by external forces. Your boyfriend may make you happy most days, but he isn't responsible for your overall happiness. Joy in your work doesn't hinge on whether your colleagues cater to your needs or your boss heaps praise on you. Your friend who is always late isn't doing that because she doesn't care about you. If you expect others to determine your self-worth and mindset, you will be disappointed. And instead of turning your disappointment into acceptance, you turn to food. When the numbing of the food wears off, we feel worse because we believe we are weak and don't have the willpower to succeed. The real problem is that we haven't actually dealt with the pain of our unmet expectations. We haven't reached acceptance, so the feelings come back tenfold.

When you become aware of your own behaviour and accept that you can't control others, you can break free from the fear-eat-regret cycle and arrive at the root of the real issue behind your eating.

UNDERSTANDING YOUR OWN MISPLACED EXPECTATIONS

Let's take a moment to explore your own expectations. You can choose something small to work with at first, but don't be afraid to repeat these questions for the bigger issues in your life as well. I recommend journaling your answers to give yourself space to explore your feelings.

1. Can you think of an expectation you have that gets repeated often and causes you pain?
2. Is there anything about this expectation that feels familiar, perhaps similar to something from your childhood or your past?
3. Consider the outcomes of this expectation. What usually happens?
4. What is the feeling that comes up for you when this expectation isn't met?
5. Can you let these feelings wash over you? How does it feel to sit with them for a moment?
6. What can you learn from these feelings?
7. How could you behave differently next time?

How might it feel to let go of this expectation? This exercise can get quite emotional, and that is okay. If you want to cry, receive the tears as you would a beloved friend. Let the waves keep washing over and stay with it, telling yourself that you are safe, you are loved, and you are worthy. You are courageous. As you feel the emotions begin to subside, just breathe deeply and let peace take over.

NO ONE IS SUGGESTING YOU SETTLE

Adopt this statement as a mantra: There is nothing wrong with high standards, but I need to accept outcomes without losing personal peace. Please do not interpret this message as I should just settle for whatever lot I've got.

When we accept other people as they are instead of trying to fast-forward them into some sort of personal growth so they treat us better, we stand in our own power. Their issues and all their "-isms" no longer affect our self-worth. They cannot provide us the authentic peace we're seeking—that sort of peace is located only deep within ourselves. We won't locate it unless we focus on our own attitude, our own perspective, and our own acceptance of what is.

This acceptance is an opportunity to heal, to grow, and to flourish.

Please don't confuse expectations with goals. Having goals in your life, whether to lose weight or have a successful relationship, is perfectly fine. But with expectations, we constantly give our power away to other people and situations that we have no control over.

What does acceptance entail? Letting go. If you're in a relationship with someone, for instance, and they're cheating on you, that is not good. So I am not suggesting that you accept that. What you might have to accept, however, is that you'll need to make a change. Maybe you will seek marital counselling or decide to leave the relationship, but the one thing we can be sure of is that you cannot change another person unless they want to change.

This form of acceptance maintains your personal dignity and self-worth. Not to mention you're saving a considerable amount of energy (and cortisol production) by not having the same arguments over and over again with someone who has never shown that they are capable of living up to your expectations.

To practice this type of acceptance, say—and believe—the following mantras:

- *I cannot change it.*
- *I will release this.*
- *I am enough, and my disappointment does not add to nor take away from that.*
- *I am safe.*
- *I am worthy of peace.*
- *Everything at this moment is okay.*

When we accept things as they are, the process of acceptance can actually bring up a lot of emotions. As human beings, we often do not want to experience uncomfortable, painful emotions. Once you arrive at a place of acceptance, however, you actually give yourself space and permission to have these feelings about the person or the situation. It has to start with you. This doesn't mean that you're not going to feel sad or grieve over it, but what it does mean is that if we allow ourselves to feel it, we're not going to constantly reach out to try and numb those feelings. The reconnection to yourself—through affirmations, breathing, meditation, even a nature walk—is worth the journey. *You* are worth the journey, and you are enough reason to take it.

MEANWHILE, BACK AT THE FRIDGE

So how do we connect the dots between acceptance and weight loss? By associating your expectations about diets (why they fail and the unresolved feelings) with the expectations you place on yourself (being able to stop eating when everything makes you want to eat). Unless you are examining the actual root cause, connecting them is not so simple.

Let's unpack some of this. First, we are looking for a quick fix that will solve everything, but diets are not sustainable because when you deprive yourself, you are undereating and not getting enough nutrition. If diets worked, everybody would be slim because it would have worked the first time—no need to hop back on the merry-go-round every few months.

Why do we keep expecting it to work? Just like there is no such thing as "just one" when we decide to eat a crisp or biscuit, there is no such thing as "this time" when it comes to finding a diet that works. If you think about it, that's a lot of expectation to put on a diet, since it cannot control your thoughts or provide you with sustainable tools to get the weight off and keep it off.

Social media has compounded this problem, because we want the lives that others post about—the beautiful photo where the beautiful people are smiling and content with their beautiful lives. No one posts about the bickering that occurred in the car when everyone was cranky and irritated before that perfect family photo was taken. We just see everyone living their best lives, and we want a part of that dream too.

The sooner we accept what's real—and the reality that diets aren't going to work—the sooner we arrive at the turning point of fixing our lives instead of fixing our diet.

If we want things to be different, we cannot stay the same and do what we've always done.

There's no magic wand to make the weight come off and stay off. This is not about starving yourself and white-knuckling it through another day where all you can think about is eating.

This is about acceptance.

Once you are *aware* that we ourselves contribute to our suffering by counting on our expectations—of others, of diets, and some of the unrealistic expectations we place on ourselves—that's the beginning of your *acceptance*. And by moving into acceptance, we begin the process of letting go of coping strategies—like over-eating—that keep our feelings at bay.

Every disappointment is an opportunity to let go of expectations. By having the courage to look inside ourselves for self-worth, we empower ourselves with the safety we've been longing for.

Our expectations are tied into what we wish would happen. Our pain is exacerbated by the wishful thinking that accompanies the pain of the unmet expectations. Whether that expectation is of a friend's behaviour or of our own ability to lose weight on the next fad diet, we are destined for disappointment when they eventually fail. As we move from awareness to acceptance, we are freeing ourselves to decide what to do with the situation that actually exists. No more treading water, hoping for rescue, because you will now have the power to rescue yourself.

SHIFT YOUR ATTITUDE, ACTIONS WILL FOLLOW

"You have two ways you can resolve this," I suggested to Jen. "Find gratitude in the ways Tom does look after you, or start taking out the rubbish yourself—but without any attitude."

As we continued our discussion, I explained to her that this doesn't mean she can't take steps to change things. "But if you don't accept things as they are, the only person that's keeping you in pain is you," I advised. "Acceptance doesn't mean you've got to like it, but by railing against it, you're giving yourself so much more suffering. By accepting it and giving it some space, you give yourself permission to have your feelings about it."

In time, things did actually change for Jen, because her attitude changed. She still wanted Tom to take out the rubbish, but by giving it some space, she could place it in proper proportion instead of tying it to her self-worth.

As she softened a bit, Jen began to notice other ways that Tom showed his love and his kindness, in ways that *he* chose. She also began to keep a gratitude list about him. The list served to remind her that if she just made the effort to treat Tom how she would really like to be treated, it took away the intensity of the rubbish battle. Eventually, Jen decided that the rubbish battle was rubbish itself and not that important—so she decided she would just handle it herself.

You can probably guess what happened next. Once Jen let go of the battle, that's when Tom stepped up.

Jen realised that the real issue was that she didn't feel cared for or noticed—and she was never going to get that from a rubbish bin. Once she consciously shifted her attention and gratitude towards the other ways that Tom loved and cared for her, Jen no longer needed to stuff down her emotions with food.

Through acceptance, we shift our focus to manage and control only what's within our own realm: namely, our thoughts, actions, and reactions. This will untangle a multitude of emotions that must be felt, expressed, and usually released. So how will you sustain this new perspective?

By responding instead of reacting.

CHAPTER 4

RESPOND, NOT REACT

When my boys were very young, ages two and four, I took them on their first plane trip. I was the lone adult on the journey, and knowing I was outnumbered, I came prepared with lots of snacks and activity magazines. It was a three-hour flight, and the first two went quietly and quite effortlessly. It looked as though I'd been worried about nothing, and somehow I even gained a third child—a little girl had joined us with our colouring.

What happened next was so sudden, I couldn't quite believe it.

My two-year-old tried to squeeze past the other two children to get to the window seat. Using his best manners, he said, "Excuse me."

Impatient, he immediately followed with three more "excuse mes," each one rising in volume, with the last one ringing loudly in our corner of the aeroplane. An older man sitting directly in front of us shot up out of his seat and bellowed, "Your children are brats!" with a voice that caught the attention of everyone within earshot. He followed up with a critique of my parenting skills and other insults that I didn't quite catch at the time, because I still couldn't fully grasp what was happening.

My adrenaline was pumping and, as it does in these heightened situations, made me a prime candidate for reacting. I knew *exactly* what I was going to say to him, and as I jumped up to deliver my snappy defence, I caught the eyes of my children looking up at me.

They were looking at me to see if their world was still safe. In this situation, they would learn more from me than from anyone else. I felt my body trying to steady itself for their sake, even though I was still very upset.

"Please don't shout at me," I said, in as calm a voice as I could muster.

This prompted the man's wife to spring up from her seat with a rolled-up newspaper and bop me on the head. Yes, this actually happened. As our eyes locked, I think she was just as surprised as I was.

I sat back down with my children and resumed colouring with them.

When we're young, we usually cannot control our default reactions to people and situations, but as adults, our job is to learn how to hit the pause button. Children are usually in reactive mode, and as adults, we have the responsibility to teach them a better way.

So far in this book, we have spent a great deal of time discussing awareness and acceptance. They both really help us understand ourselves and our place in the world. Awareness and acceptance are foundational to the success of the phase we are moving towards, where we learn how to respond instead of react.

When I look back at that incident on the plane, I realise that at some point, all of us have played each of the roles I described:

- We have been the children, who are absorbing the scene.
- We have been the man and his wife, shouting and out of control.
- We have also had our wits about us enough to stop and think before speaking.

This chapter contains practical tools about how to hit your personal pause button long enough to be aware of what's happening, accept it, and change your mindset to respond more thoughtfully. This one key step will help you in all areas of life, but especially with how you approach food.

You've probably already guessed that it requires dealing with the root causes of your issues. We have already talked about how to get to a point of acceptance. Now, it's time to put your acceptance into action. We want to respond, rather than react.

WHAT DOES A REACTION LOOK LIKE?

A reaction is immediate and rash. When we react to something, we're not thinking before speaking. We don't consider the impact of what we're about to say, and our quick temper very often throws fuel on the fire.

When we think about why we react impulsively to certain triggers, it's likely because we are already stressed. Something happens that makes us angry or upset, and we immediately react in such a way that it almost bypasses the brain. The words escape before we know it.

Social media is a great example of this phenomenon. We have all seen posts where we notice other people having an emotional reaction to the text. Scroll down the comments, and we see someone else reacting with unkind words, blaming, shaming, and angry...Their fingers have typed out the message before they've really taken a moment to process what it says. It's plain to see that this reaction was immediate and emotional. Perhaps they will not be proud of it later. Then, someone else reacts to their comment and leaves a reply just as immediate and emotional as the other. Before you know it, there's an angry, sometimes nonsensical fight in full public view, often among individuals who do not even know each other.

We have all been there. We have reacted in anger, said something we didn't mean, and done something we wished we hadn't. This is the danger of reaction: it's so easy to do, yet impossible to undo later.

A strong emotional reaction doesn't necessarily have to occur in real-time, either. You could instead react to a memory from long ago. It could just be you in a room by yourself, thinking of a past event, and then *boom*. You are triggered, and before you've even thought about it, you are eating without control, trying to feel better. It just happens. Nothing is thought through—it's just fight or flight mode, and we're fighting with food as our shield.

When our eating is in reaction to a particular triggering event, we are eating without filter and without considering the implications. We are not discriminating about what we consume, nor how much. We just know we need to numb our pain and wonder if this time, it will go away. When it doesn't, we heap more guilt and shame on ourselves for hoping that it would, since our eating has never successfully fought off our pain before.

WHAT DOES A RESPONSE LOOK LIKE?

Conversely, *responding* means considering the consequences of your actions. When you opt to respond instead of react, you have pushed through or restrained your immediate impulse in order to return to your right mind. For those of us who were brought up in a very reactive household, we rarely learn this skill, especially if the adults were always kicking off around you. How can we learn it now?

First, take notice when something triggers you. What is the physical reaction from your body? Heat? Loss of breath? Heart beating faster? Sweaty? Lump in the throat? Can you feel the adrenaline coursing through you? Just taking a few seconds to pause helps you identify the immediate reactive emotions and gives you time to breathe. This can make all the difference in what happens next.

Responding does require far more effort than reacting, because you have to consider the consequences of your choices. When you take the time to name the emotion you're experiencing, you're identifying it for what it is and putting it in its proper place. You're giving yourself the chance to learn about your feelings and become more skilled at managing them.

And then you can get on with your life.

Responding instead of reacting is a skill that takes time to develop. To make it easier, I've broken it down into what I call the PEACE process:

- **Pause:** As soon as you notice that you are triggered and begin to experience an emotional response, hit the pause button. Sometimes, adrenaline can race through us, and we need a few moments to be able to think straight. So plan an escape route: walk away, count to ten, do some slow breathing. Remind yourself that you are not subject to your feelings.
- **Evaluate:** Try your best to evaluate the emotion you're caught up in at that moment. Are you feeling resentful, lonely, hurt, despairing, vulnerable, or maybe a combination of these? Connecting with yourself and naming that emotion helps you to become an impartial observer of yourself. Naming the emotion strips it of its power over you and allows you to step out of the whirlwind of the moment.
- **Acknowledge:** When we acknowledge our hurt and the source of it, we improve our chances of not getting stuck in it. Acknowledgement of what triggered the emotion helps you remove yourself from it. As soon as you step outside of yourself to observe, you're already once removed from it. What is it that has *actually* triggered you? Was there something going on beneath the surface or before the impulse?
- **Choose:** When we react rashly, we do so without thinking about the consequences. By contrast, choosing your response means taking consequences into account. When you are reminded of your goals and what you want to achieve, your response has a better chance to align with that goal in a kind, thoughtful way.

- **Empower:** Once you have made the choice to respond, the final step is to act. You are empowered to act in the way that is best for you, whether responding to others or your own issues. When we take ownership of our responses, we are taking a powerful step towards healing and letting go. It's empowering!

As we practice PEACE, it slowly becomes easier to trust ourselves. Learning how to respond thoughtfully takes time, but when you choose to respond to another person, yourself, or an event with love and kindness, you have taken a courageous step—one that is forward-moving and healing.

Remember to be kind to yourself, because this is a process. Much like a toddler learning to walk, you'll stumble a bit to find your footing. The steps will feel awkward and new. You can't place the expectation on yourself to suddenly be perfect at this, but it will get better with time. PEACE is within your grasp.

PRACTICAL TIPS FOR THE PAUSE

The ability to figure out your triggers only comes when you take the time to pause. If you want to respond and not react, you need a break. Like a breath of fresh air, it can make all the difference. Here are some practical ways to accomplish this:

- Breathe deeply
- Leave the room
- Avoid speaking
- Avoid nonverbal aggression (eye-rolling, arms crossed, clenching your jaw, and so on)
- Calmly say, "Let me get back to you" or "I need a moment"

MAKING PEACE WITH FOOD

Why so much emphasis on response? Because it has a direct effect on your eating.

When you're feeling upset because someone didn't call or feeling like you are not good enough, it's easy to slip into reaction mode instead of thoughtfully responding. That's when you reach for the food, unaware of the *real* reason you're upset. Or if you're aware of what triggered you, you don't care. You just want the pain to subside, and in that moment, you eat.

It doesn't even have to be a major heartbreak or epic argument that triggers you. Maybe it's something as simple as dropping your children off at school and noticing a group of parents chatting together nearby. They look so chummy together, having a wonderful time—without you. The uncomfortable feeling that you're being ignored graduates to a fear of being left out, and this swiftly builds into despair that you'll never truly belong. When you arrive back home, you start with the children's leftovers from breakfast, then their after-school treats, then whatever else you can find so you don't have to sit with your painful feelings.

And after you react by eating, you only feel worse.

Meanwhile, back at the school, the parents chatting have no idea what you're feeling or that you didn't feel comfortable joining them.

Whatever the situation, this is not about other people. This is about *your* feelings and what's going on in *your* life.

So when we make PEACE with our eating, we are choosing to

respond rather than react to moments big and small. When we react, we think that food is the solution to make us feel better, but it just makes us feel worse. Then we get this emotional hang-over about what we have just done, which sends us back to the food. But when we pause, we let the sanity back in. We can make a different choice this time. We can feel the food calling us, but we choose to do something different by using these tools.

When we press the pause button, we can stave off the emotional cravings until the desire to eat passes. It gives us space that we need to make thoughtful choices and consider the consequences of each possible choice.

When you think about reaching for something to eat, wait five minutes. If that's too difficult, just do it for sixty seconds, just to get some space. If you can get through sixty seconds, you know you can go another sixty seconds. Set a timer and say to yourself:

· *I am aware that I'm now in this reaction mode, wanting to hit the food.*
· *I am going to press the pause button for sixty seconds.*
· *Since I made it through sixty seconds, I'm going to try pausing for another sixty seconds.*

And keep going until the urge passes. While you're in that space—the pause—you can do something really kind and caring for yourself, like:

· Put on some music and dance
· Call a friend or loved one
· Do a three- or five-minute meditation
· Play with your dog

- Brush your teeth
- Say a prayer
- Do some star jumps
- Watch a funny video
- Play solitaire

I also find it helpful to engage in some positive self-talk in these moments to offer some encouragement. Try repeating some affirmations or mantras:

- *I nourish my mind, body, and heart with a loving heart.*
- *I will be patient even in the midst of trouble.*
- *I will not be hard on myself today.*
- *I treat my body with loving kindness.*

Using these ideas, build up to a pause of sixty seconds, then two minutes, and so on, until you reach five minutes. The idea is to get yourself in a place where you are more mindful about giving yourself permission to eat the food, but wait for five minutes. Even if you *do* choose to eat after your mindful pause, you have shown yourself that it's *possible* to make a different choice.

When your time is up, think about what your motive is at that moment. What are you wanting to numb, punish, or control with your emotions? If you still decide to eat, what is your motive right then, and how does it relate to the food? *You do not have to be a slave to your impulses.*

Finally, respond by thinking through:

- *What do I need right now?*
- *What am I really craving right now?*

- *How am I going to feel once I have eaten it?*

When it comes to food, you've got to accept that you have a problem and that you keep doing something that keeps you in misery. But once you become aware of that and accept it, you can take a different path. If you can just give a bit of time to think about those things, it will get easier. For now, focus on making these small shifts, which ultimately make all the difference. Make different choices until you can make the choice not to eat. You will find your real, authentic, essential self is still there, underneath the layers you have built up over the years.

ONE MOMENT AT A TIME

When we are not directly involved in a situation, it's easy to identify who is in reactive mode—but it's not as easy when we ourselves are caught in the situation. That's why responding is so important. The implications reach beyond ourselves; they affect our relationships, our contributions in the world, and our experiences.

And after getting bopped on the head with the newspaper that day, I also learned our choice to respond can literally and figuratively affect our freedom.

Following the newspaper bop heard round the plane, I sat back down. After some intense colouring to work out my own aggression, I looked up and saw the other passengers smiling at me. The couple sitting behind me had teenage sons, and all three were playing peek-a-boo quietly with the boys. I took the little girl back to her parents, who were in ignorant bliss at the front of the plane. The rest of the flight went quietly without incident… until we exited.

After making the required stop off at the loo for the boys, the older lady—the one with the newspaper—was waiting for me. She looked at me, shamefaced, and said, "Here's a magazine that was under our seats. I think it belongs to your children."

"Thank you," I replied, and went on to the luggage carousel.

Before I had a chance to look for our bags, a man and woman approached us, and the man showed me his badge, just like they do in the movies. He was an air marshal, and the woman was his assistant.

"We were seated five rows ahead of you," he explained, "and just want to thank you for diffusing the situation." The moment the man started shouting, the marshall had radioed through to the airport and the police were waiting. "In the confined space of an aeroplane, situations can escalate extremely quickly."

"I am a mother myself, and I hadn't heard either of your boys make any noise until that moment," his assistant added. "If someone had insulted my children like that, I would have to say something."

The air marshall said that when he'd finished the call, he was just about to get out of the seat and intervene. When I simply sat down, he said, he'd never seen that before.

"Well, when she bopped me on the head with a newspaper," I said. "I thought it was best to sit down."

He looked at me very seriously and said, "I'm so sorry. I had no idea *that* had happened. If I had been aware of that, the couple would have been taken to the front of the plane and handcuffed to their seats."

Well well! I thought to myself, rather pleased. *Not only have I saved two elderly people from being dragged to the front of the plane and handcuffed, but I also managed to divert an international incident.*

As I was busy high-fiving myself in my mind, another thought crept in. *I could have easily told them what I thought of that behaviour. I could have wagged my finger, and even given a firm little poke to the newspaper bopper. And I, too, could have been taken to the front of the plane in handcuffs, in front of my children.*

Yes, it could have been a different outcome. Never have I ever been more grateful that I responded, and not reacted.

As the marshall said, situations can escalate quickly. This is true of our emotions as well, and before we know it, we're eating an entire minibar (or whatever your personal minibar incident involves). Choosing to respond instead of react is a process.

I may have made progress that day, but I still have moments where I react rather than respond. The difference is that now I know to treat myself with kindness. As you practice awareness with the PEACE method, you'll recognise the triggers and feel more in control over your responses to them. In time, it will get easier—and this practice will position you to take action towards the sort of change that moves you past the internal wars you've been fighting your whole life.

CHAPTER 5

PRACTISING GRATITUDE

Tasha was a client of mine who was doing excellent work. We had been working together for twelve weeks, and her goal was to lose forty pounds.

She had already lost twenty-five, and she was feeling quite confident about her choices and her new-found freedom with food. She was on top of the world.

But then, one day, Tasha's accountability form was late.

I always require my clients to complete a quick form outlining their wins, challenges, and lessons learned over the past week. It's a great tool to stay mindful between our meetings, and it helps keep my clients on track with their goals.

So when Tasha's form went missing, I reached out.

She didn't need to say anything—I knew from her tone that

she had fallen back into the fear-eat-regret cycle. I could feel the heartbreak through the phone as she told me what had happened.

One weekend trip with a group of old girlfriends, and all of Tasha's new skills went out the window.

The first night began as girls' nights often do, with a glass of wine. Her friends had complimented her weight loss, and Tasha was feeling wonderful. She decided that one slice of cake and some chocolate wouldn't hurt, so she indulged along with the rest of her friends.

But then it wasn't just one. Tasha kept going back for more. Each time she entered the kitchen, she would slice another sliver of cake that went straight into her mouth, no plate needed—and she didn't even enjoy it. When the group ordered takeaway, *wham!* Tasha was ordering food and puddings like it was her last supper.

The next morning, Tasha awoke feeling that she had ruined everything. All her hard work went straight down the drain. Feeling very ashamed, she thought, *What does anything matter anymore?* When she arrived home, she carried on eating everything in sight, feeling like she was undoing all her good work with every bite. For three days, Tasha ate in secret, unable to stop the fear-eat-regret cycle as she rode the spiral of pain downward.

By the time she spoke with me over the phone, she was distraught. "Did I ruin the last few months? Am I a lost cause?"

Pausing to breathe between sobs, Tasha choked out, "This is the worst possible thing I could have done."

This type of self-sabotage is common. I've experienced it many times, and surely you have, too. It's painful, but it can also be one of your greatest learning tools—if you'll allow it to be.

"Okay," I replied. "Let's talk about gratitude for a moment."

At that moment, Tasha was in full-tilt self-loathing. The last thing that she was feeling was gratitude. But sometimes the last thing we feel like doing is the thing that ultimately changes our perspective.

"What if that moment gave you insight into preventing you from overeating again?" I asked. "What if this was an opportunity to change things? How could you do things differently next time?"

Remember, it's the *regret* that sends us back to the food. It's only in our awareness and acceptance of that regret that we can move forward. And gratitude, it turns out, is an incredible tool to help us get to that acceptance.

I asked her, "What if you could accept where you are because there is something to be learnt that could transform your perspective to the point you are actually grateful for it?"

The sniffles stopped. She was listening.

I asked Tasha to sit down and, for forty minutes, write down everything that she was grateful for in the last three months—the time we'd been working together. Some of the items she came up with included making wiser choices when eating out, not going back to the fridge after dinner, not grazing all day, and not finishing the food left on her children's plates.

From there, I asked her to write down everything that she was grateful for in her life. Finally, I asked her to write what she was grateful for about the fear-eat-regret cycle that she had just experienced.

It took her an hour to complete the exercise, but when we spoke about it the following week, Tasha's desperation had been replaced with gratitude. Not only was she back on track, but she said that every time she prepared and ate her beautiful meals, she felt grateful. She was grateful for her progress, and grateful for not being back in that place where she hated herself.

It took a couple of weeks, but Tasha eventually even found gratitude for her weekend of eating, because she realised that, with this experience, she was better prepared to do things differently next time. Because there's always a next time.

Today, Tasha's daily gratitude practice includes adding to the list of things she's thankful for. She does this each morning before breakfast, and she completes the exercise as though her life depended on it.

And in a way, it does.

Acceptance teaches us that it's not what happens that matters—it's your attitude about it. One of the best ways to embrace your life as it is right now is to cultivate a practice of gratitude. Gratitude is the first and simplest action to take. It enables you to move forward with your life and embrace peace. Gratitude is the bridge between acceptance and the subsequent actions you will take to move past the food and reclaim your life, because it's the step that changes your outlook and moves you towards even greater change.

WHAT IS GRATITUDE?

As human beings, we are designed for community and a shared sense of responsibility to help ourselves, help others, and make our world a better place. Gratitude is a deep sense of thankfulness that reminds us that we are not our own islands. Therefore, the practice of gratitude requires a certain amount of humility and thoughtfulness. We must pause to take inventory of our lives and remember the little things that often get overlooked in the busy-ness of our days—and then make a conscious choice to no longer take them for granted. Gratitude is not necessarily forward-thinking as much as it is a renewed thinking; when we look back at what we have often taken for granted, we are giving ourselves the opportunity to be thankful for what we missed and make the decision to no longer overlook these gifts. We have the power to make this choice. We can choose to be grateful or not—it's all in the attitude.

Too often, we think that losing weight, earning a certain amount of money, or finding the right person has to happen before we can consider our lives to be "right." On the contrary: gratitude is something we need in our present, right now. By focusing on what's good in our lives and being thankful for what we do have, our eyes are opened to even more that's already right in our lives. This makes it much easier to reach acceptance, because our problems are balanced—and perhaps even overshadowed—by all the wonderful things around us that we've begun to focus on.

Being grateful gives us time to stop, reflect, and be present.

Gratitude is *not* about denying the difficulties you may experience or an expectation that you put a positive spin on everything.

But it is about opening our hearts, even during a crisis, because this is when we have the most to gain. When we feel broken, having a grateful perspective on our lives can heal us. And when we feel real despair, gratitude can give us hope—so long as we have been nurturing it. We can't just will ourselves to feel grateful, nor will happy feelings come from our expectations of the world and others.

When tapping into gratitude, it's important to keep our hearts open, and it takes courage to do that. We want to be happy, to be loved, to belong, and to connect to other people, which requires a certain amount of vulnerability. By taking control of your perceptions and filtering them through the lens of gratitude, you have better control over your thoughts and actions. There will be less "mind chatter" that skews your expectations and perceptions. By being more present and loving with gratitude, you are more reasonable, more resilient, and more objective.

Gratitude also connects us to everything in the world: other people, nature, ourselves, as well as to joy and peace. This connection to the good things is the opposite of isolation, which breeds bad feelings, resentment, and very often the urge to reach for food.

Gratitude works because—unlike the fear-worry-eat-regret cycle—it creates an *upward* spiral that continues to lift your spirits a little higher each time you practice it. The truth is that wherever you focus your attention, the object of your attention expands in importance. The more obsessed we are with food, the more we think about it—and thought leads to action. But if we learn to replace thoughts of food with thoughts of gratitude, we change the entire direction of our lives.

The more you focus on the good things, the more good things you will notice. It won't just happen overnight, and it does take a bit of work. Bit by bit, the practice of gratitude builds a precious foundation of good things, and your life will change for the better because you are looking out for them and protecting them instead of taking them for granted.

Even if you're sceptical of this effect, try practising gratitude for four weeks. Science has proven that four weeks of practising gratitude can create amazing results and rewire your brain.[2] There is also proof that practising gratitude improves health, longevity, and healing when we're sick. Gratitude also helps to decompress and de-stress us.[3]

GRATITUDE AND WEIGHT LOSS

I have worked with clients who are desperate to lose weight but say that they are not overeating. When they keep a journal that records absolutely everything that goes into their mouths—even one tiny teaspoon of peanut butter or a single jelly bean—they finally see how much of their eating occurs mindlessly throughout the day. It adds up to a lot!

It is precisely this black hole of mindless eating that gratitude can address. As we move to a place where we regularly practice gratitude, we become much more mindful. In moments of gratitude, we are paying careful attention to how we are living.

2   Robert A. Emmons and Michael E. McCullough, *The Psychology of Gratitude* (New York: Oxford University Press, 2004).

3   Christian T. Gloria and Mary A. Steinhardt, "Relationships among Positive Emotions, Coping, Resilience and Mental Health," *Stress and Health* 32, no. 2 (2014): 145-156, https://doi.org/10.1002/smi.2589.

We take time to stop, reflect, and review the details of our lives with sensitivity and compassion.

As we learned in our exploration of awareness and acceptance, we have to notice what we are doing in order to move on and change. Overeating is rooted in misplaced self-loathing; if you can begin to love yourself, find things that you like about yourself, and be grateful for all of it, you will value yourself more. When you place more value in yourself, you will want to look after yourself instead of punishing your body with food.

By design, gratitude provides a moment to pause. It increases our ability to wait, increases our patience, and gives us space to be kind to ourselves. In turn, we are less likely to look towards food as the solution to feel better.

There was a time in my life when I wouldn't express my emotions. I would just push them down, along with food, unaware of what I was doing. Because I had numbed my awareness, I did it all the time, often mindlessly—whilst watching the television, cooking, and so on. There was this constant need to fill the void, but once I learned how to take the pause, gratitude was a gateway to change.

There is a peace that emerges when you feel truly grateful for what you have. Gratitude is a wonderful tool to stop you reaching for the food—because otherwise, that reaching will only lead you to more pain. When we practice gratitude, we have an opportunity to extend more compassion to ourselves and begin to open up to the life we are truly meant to live.

HOW TO FIND GRATITUDE

To be clear, real gratitude is not the Pollyanna principle of putting a positive spin on everything. That type of forced positivity can actually cause you more pain. I'm talking about finding gratitude that is authentic to *you*.

That said, the idea of practising gratitude may feel awkward at first. Start really small, with those things that lift the mood or brighten your day: a parking space, your bed, your home, a glass of clean water, a child's smile, the graceful way a tree blows in the wind, a bird singing—all the little details that we often overlook.

Actively looking for things to be grateful for can take a bit of work. When we take time to notice, however, we are creating an awareness of our surroundings, and this awareness is key to a healthy life. As we get better at our practice, even the darkest days will contain small glimmers of hope and gratitude.

If you've been concentrating on your trials and tribulations for a long time, practising gratitude will give you the opportunity to look at your life with fresh eyes. In many cases, it may feel as though you are truly seeing some of it for the first time!

To jump-start your practice, here are some ideas to ponder and questions to ask yourself:

- Take a moment each evening to evaluate your day. What, or who, has made you happy today? (Nothing is too small—if you smelled a flower and it brought you joy, it counts!)
- Go through the alphabet and find something that you are grateful for that starts with each letter.
- Set a timer for three minutes and see how many things you

can recall that you are grateful for. Speak these aloud; put them out into the universe.

- Keep a gratitude journal and write down things you are grateful for. On days that seem dark, open it up and read past entries to remind yourself that you have a lot going for you.
- Look around your room, wherever you are. What do you see that are you grateful for? A book, your bed, your clothes, your blankets? Make a mental list and say a quick word of thanks for each of them.
- Focus on your senses. What can you see that you're grateful for? What can you smell? What can you touch that you're grateful for? What do you taste that you're grateful for?
- Think about someone you love—a family member, a friend, a spouse, a companion. What are you grateful for with regard to that particular person?
- Keep a jar and a small notepad where you can write little notes of gratitude when the mood strikes. Drop each note into the jar to create a visual reminder each time you see it that you have a growing pile of things that are good in your life. You can always pick a couple out of your jar to start the day by reminding yourself what you are grateful for.
- Try something new. Maybe it was scary, maybe you weren't great at it, but you stepped out of your comfort zone. That, alone, is something to be grateful for.
- If someone has inspired you, show your gratitude. You can write them a letter to express how much they mean to you and then, if possible, arrange to meet up and actually read it to them. This can have a profound effect on both you and the recipient of your gratitude.
- If someone has challenged you, find a way to be grateful for the growth opportunity—especially if you were able to respond and not react.

As you experiment with your gratitude practice, not all of the suggestions above will feel right for you—and that's fine. Use the prompts that resonate and let go of anything that doesn't serve you. This is a personal practice, and the important thing is that you find a way to reflect daily on all the things you are grateful for. The benefits are enormous.

CHERISH YOURSELF

Once you have found things in the external world to be grateful for, it's time to shift that focus inward. It's important to cherish *yourself* by being grateful for what you are, what you have accomplished, and who you are as a human being.

Try these prompts to get started being grateful for your own amazing self:

- Think about the work you have done on awareness and acceptance as you've read this book. Be grateful that you are doing the difficult work to feel your feelings for the sake of your health.
- How do you earn a living? Be grateful for the abilities and talents that support you in this way.
- Name three things you accomplished today, even if one of them was simply making your bed. Acknowledge that *you get things done.*
- Are you a good friend to others? Be grateful that you are viewed as someone they can count on.
- Have you achieved a goal or won an award? You are not an imposter—say out loud, "I did this."
- What happened today that brought you one step closer to healing yourself from a relationship or memory? Be grateful for that one step.

- Acknowledge a kindness you extended to someone, even if it's just a smile you offered to them, or that you opened a door for a stranger.
- Which body parts are you constantly criticising? Find a way to be grateful for them. For example, instead of hating your thighs, be grateful for legs that can take you places.

Self-compassion takes practice, because we are not used to seeing it or giving it to ourselves.

It's really easy to put ourselves down when we're not feeling good about who we are, and this is especially true when you have extra weight to lose. Don't wait until your life is perfect or your body is perfect before you practice gratitude, or you will wait out the rest of your life, sidelined. It can feel quite strange to let your own light shine, but learn to cherish yourself by virtue of simply being *you*. It's an incredible gift.

THE DAILY DISCIPLINE OF GRATITUDE

Since the research shows gratitude can make a real difference in four weeks' time, I'd like you to commit to a month-long gratitude practice. But how do we hold ourselves *accountable* as we build a daily gratitude practice?

Many people will set a reminder on their mobile phones to take two minutes a day to pause and be grateful. Others review their gratitude lists when they brush their teeth in the morning and again just before bed.

You can find your own way to get into this habit, but it will be more powerful when you make it a part of your daily routine. Two minutes a day add up to one hour over a four-week period. It won't cost you a thing, but the change that will occur is priceless.

When you begin to notice how good gratitude feels, you're encouraged to do it again—more often, and for longer periods of time—because this is something that works when you do it on a daily basis. It's not as effective twice a week, or every other day. Two minutes a day, *every day*, yields beautiful outcomes and eventually becomes second-nature.

You can also enlist the help of a "gratitude buddy" to help keep your new habit on track. All you need to do is set aside a few minutes a day to discuss what you're thankful for with a spouse, child, or friend. Sometimes, I'll go for a walk with a friend and we'll each discuss three things we are grateful for in our lives. But you don't necessarily have to share what you've come up with for this to be effective. At minimum, just send a text to say that you have done your daily gratitude practice to keep you accountable. No matter how you approach it, enlisting a gratitude buddy to be your accountability partner adds another layer of support—as well as joy.

Gratitude can change your life by changing the way you perceive it. It stops the self-pity and victim mentality and replaces it with happiness and positivity. It puts us on an upward spiral in which good feelings grow and expand. Gratitude is the first step—and an easy one—towards lasting change.

UNEXPECTED GRATITUDE

Practising gratitude isn't always easy, especially when we are dealing with difficult people and situations. But it's when you find yourself struggling that gratitude is most powerful.

When you are irritated, you're in the danger zone for turning to food as a temporary solution for your problems. When these feelings come up, pause and ask yourself what the source of your irritation is. Is it someone at work? One of your kids? Your spouse? Or is it a particular situation rather than a person?

Once you've named the source of your feelings, immediately sit down and write a list of five things you're *grateful* for when you think about this person or situation. It may feel challenging at first, but this exercise can help you quickly regain perspective—*before* you head to the fridge for some comfort food.

EVEN THE DETOURS WILL GET YOU THERE

I'll end this chapter with the same questions I asked Tasha to consider as we worked through her setback: what happens when we accept where we are, even when things aren't going our way, but we can learn from the experience?

You cultivate that acceptance by learning to incorporate gratitude throughout your day. This is why the daily gratitude list Tasha writes each morning is so important to her. If she felt a hiccup in her day that had her glancing at the fridge, she would go back and refer to her list until the moment passed.

If you find yourself slipping back into victim mode, pause and think: *What am I grateful for in this exact moment?* You will actually *feel* the shift, because you can't hold on to gratitude and stress at the same time.

Once you *really* see how your life is changing, you're encouraged to carry on and make more lifestyle changes—including self-care changes that help you lose weight. I'm not talking about diets here. I'm talking about the changes you have made from within, where you actually begin to *feel* and *see* outcomes that put you on an upward trajectory instead of a downward spiral.

Make space for the inevitable mistakes and off days. When the proverbial hits the fan and you turn to food, you might think there is no gratitude found there, but what have you learned from that slip-up that inspires you to handle it differently next time? Those detours are meaningful, so practice self-compassion when they occur. Instead of beating yourself up, you can turn to your gratitude practice to find the good even in your mistakes.

Be grateful for those times, because they serve as reminders of how bad you have felt in the past and remind you to no longer take for granted the good things in your life. Keep walking in gratitude. You are taking yourself to a far more loving place.

CHAPTER 6

EXTREME SELF-CARE

When my mother died after a short illness, I was also going through a very difficult time with my husband; in fact, we separated for a period. My children were both under the age of three, and I was only sleeping a few hours here and there.

My day would start around five in the morning, holding an infant with one hand and a toddler with the other while trying to get them fed and changed. Instead of having a proper meal, I would graze their leftovers or grab something quick as I rushed out the door to get to the park. I would arrive home exhausted, feeling lonely, and mindlessly reach for something else to eat before even attempting to start the never-ending chores.

I was running on empty all the time. There was a constant heaviness with what was going on in my life, and there was no time left to grieve the loss of my mother or process the separation from my husband—and certainly no time for myself.

I felt completely squeezed out of my own life. I was constantly chasing my tail, not having enough time to prepare good food for myself, and reaching for sugary, quick fixes for the energy—all the while piling on the pounds.

This routine would lead me to big insulin crashes, which in turn led me to crave even more sugary quick-fixes to try to keep my energy up. I was absolutely wired by the time I went to bed, even though I was totally exhausted. My mind was like a washing machine churning through all my problems and grief: round and round, pulsating, spinning, and unable to shut off. Then, beginning at five the next morning, I would get up and repeat the cycle. On the outside, all appeared to be fine. Once the door was closed, I was alone with my pain.

This wasn't the life I wanted for myself or my children. It was crystal clear to me that I needed to make changes in my life—and I couldn't wait for someone or something else to make it happen.

It had to begin with me.

PUT ON YOUR OWN OXYGEN MASK FIRST

We often overcomplicate self-care by assuming it's some sort of luxury not available to us, but the truth is that self-care is actually quite simple. It's making time to take care of yourself mentally, emotionally, and physically. No one is going to make that time for you, however—that's the difficult part. You have to do it for yourself. That requires you to acknowledge and accept that you are valuable and just as worthy as anyone else to receive nurturing and care.

There is a reason the flight attendants tell you to put your own oxygen mask on before you assist a child with theirs. If you are out cold, you are no help to your child. You have to look after yourself first. The same rule applies to self-care. It helps your mood, your thought patterns, and your wellbeing. And only once we heal ourselves are we capable of healthy connections with others.

Many of us didn't receive proper care, nurturing, and cherishing as children. We carry this into adulthood, feeling less deserving of life's gifts and beauty. We operate in ways that are fueled by our insecurity. As a result, we do not give ourselves the sort of care that, ironically, we are more than willing to give to others. In fact, the whole concept of self-care can be a bit wobbly for us at first. It can feel uncomfortable and downright selfish. We second-guess our actions, thinking, *Am I being selfish? Am I being self-centred? Do I deserve this?* Recognise that this may be a carry-over from the care you didn't receive as a child.

Self-care is actually quite the opposite of selfishness. It's a step towards really acknowledging your precious self. When we wait for a knight in shining armour to look after us or fantasise about how winning the lottery will change our life, we're waiting for the wrong thing. We must be our own knight. The care we give ourselves produces a ripple effect that permeates other areas of our lives: we become better spouses, parents, and friends. We become a better version of ourselves.

We can begin right now, today, to show kindness to ourselves. The goal of extreme self-care is to become your own best friend. When we show up for ourselves first, we can offer a far better version of ourselves to those whom we love. Our self-care begins with three key components to health: sleep, relaxation, and joy.

SLEEP

Sleep is one of the most important components of self-care. Most of us shrug it off either because a good night's sleep remains elusive or we think we'll "catch up" on our sleep some other day. Sleep is undervalued, yet it affects just about everything in our lives.

We all know that inadequate sleep makes us irritable and affects our energy levels. It also affects our ability to think straight. When we are sleep-deprived, we are not able to make good decisions, which may lead us to make poor food choices—the type of eating that can easily set off the fear-eat-regret cycle and lead to feelings of shame. Inadequate sleep also affects our immune system and makes us more susceptible to illness. So much of our health depends upon a good night's sleep that the missing hours can quickly send us into a downward spiral of poor outcomes.

A lack of sleep also affects your hormonal system. In particular, being sleep-deprived causes leptin levels to drop quite dramatically. Leptin is the appetite hormone that sends a signal to your brain to tell your body you are full, so losing sleep can lead directly to eating more. We all know this feeling: when you haven't slept well, cravings go up, no food quite hits the spot, and it never feels like you've eaten enough. Your body is literally working against your weight loss, all because you haven't enjoyed adequate rest.

RELAXATION

Most of the time, we don't even realise how stressed we are. Don't believe me? Wherever you are right now, take a deep breath. As you exhale, really try to relax and notice if your shoulders go down. Did your shoulders just lower by a couple of inches? We can hold so much stress internally without even realising it, and the shoulder area is one of the places it commonly resides.

Stress builds up slowly throughout the day: bills, work, deadlines, traffic jams, getting the kids to school, emails, and laundry all add up. As your to-do list gets longer, the stress hormone known as cortisol will inch up along with it. Cortisol is a built-in survival mechanism our bodies produce when we are stressed. In the ancient past, it helped us run away from predators and kept us safe.

Thousands of years later, cortisol is not as helpful—our bodies don't know the difference between a sabre toothed tiger on the attack and a looming deadline. Our body thinks we are about to run for our lives, so the last thing we need at that moment is to digest food. Instead, the cortisol sends the message to the brain: produce adrenaline, we need to run fast!

Only we're not running; we're just trying to get through our day. So somewhere between the cortisol's message and the adrenaline rush, our body holds on to the fat because it thinks we may need it for survival—which is why you get the muffin top around the middle. That is a stress tummy.

And unlike our ancestors who could relax after escaping that predator, our stress can be constant. Chronic stress means our cortisol levels remain elevated, which has adverse effects on our entire body. A bit of precious time each day to relax will bring enormous benefits to both body and spirit.

JOY

Joy is deeply personal and satisfying. As children, we were naturally playful—fun and laughter came easily. Joy is abundant in young children, who will stop and marvel at a flower, touching it gently. They're happy with a bit of water and sand to make all sorts of fabulous sculptures. So when did all of this stop?

When we reconnect with ourselves, we have an opportunity to mentally de-clutter. We can return to what brings us joy, and even perhaps discover new joys. When we do things that we love, we bring out the best parts of ourselves. Think back to what brought you joy as a child. For me, it was netball—so I joined a netball group in my forties. We were all about the same age, and local mums. As a team, we might not have set the netball world on fire, but it was an hour of fun and connection, with the added benefit of moving our bodies and making a few more friends.

Joy benefits us personally—and when it does, it overflows into the rest of our life. Make it a self-care goal to find your personal joy, and let it expand naturally when you do.

EXTREME SELF-CARE AND WEIGHT LOSS

What does all of this have to do with weight loss? For starters, all three aspects of self-care—sleep, relaxation, and joy—have a direct effect on both our attitude towards food and our food choices.

We have already touched on the evolutionary point of view of stress as a mechanism designed to help you survive. In times of stress, your body isn't all that interested in burning excess fat, because it's in survival mode. Your caveman ancestors might have needed any extra pounds as an insurance policy against scarcity later. In modern days, when small, incremental things build up to a lot of daily stress, the body is still designed to hold on to the weight. Cortisol kicks in and doesn't back down, keeping your body on high alert to hang on to every last ounce you can for future use.

The overall effect is that the body is then unable to get to a state of relaxation. You're constantly fighting against chronic low-level stress, which takes energy away from your metabolic ability to burn fat.

While stress wreaks havoc on our digestion, joy produces the opposite effect. On a scientific level, we feel joy in our brain's neurotransmitters, which are also responsible for processes in almost every aspect of our body, from blood flow to digestion. Unlikely as it may sound, our digestive system is closely linked with our mood. The gut and brain are constantly talking to and influencing each other, which is why it's not surprising that anxiety often goes hand-in-hand with digestive issues like irritable bowel syndrome (IBS).[4]

Engaging in self-care helps to correct us at a physiological level by substituting joy for stress and helping our bodies heal from being on high alert all the time. Self-care also helps us deal with the root cause of our eating. As we know, it's often not hunger that makes us turn to food, but a deep longing from within, a void that never seems to be filled. We know all too well that stress is a major trigger that makes us reach out for food.

4   Stefan-Lucian Popa and Dan Lucian Dumitrascu. "Anxiety and IBS Revisited: Ten Years Later," *Medicine and Pharmacy Reports* 88. no. 3 (2015): 253–257. https://doi.org/10.15386/cjmed-495.

When we realise that our cravings have less to do with food and more to do with what is going on *within,* we can change our lives. Joy makes us present and enables us to live in the moment. It also takes away the mind chatter, the obsessiveness, and the negative self-talk. Joy helps us connect to ourselves and to others.

HOW TO GET STARTED WITH EXTREME SELF-CARE

So, how do we get there? I mean, how many of us really *don't* want to get a better night's sleep? Or to relax? Or feel joy? Most of us want that, but getting there is the challenge. The good news is that you can start right now to provide the deep, nurturing care that you need in your life.

TIPS FOR BETTER SLEEP

When it comes to sleep, treat yourself as you would prepare a small child for bed. Children thrive on calming bedtime routines, and you will too. Ideally, you should stop eating two hours before bedtime, and allow yourself at least one hour to prepare for sleep. The following suggestions will also help, so long as you make them habits:

- Take a warm bath before bed.
- Lower the overhead lights a bit earlier, or turn them off and just use lamps.
- Try white noise. An app or white noise machine provides soothing sounds of the ocean or rain that will lull you to sleep.
- Set a bedtime and a wake-up time that is consistent every day—even on weekends! It's much easier for your body to get high-quality sleep when you're on a schedule.

- Cool your bedroom down to eighteen degrees centigrade. It takes your body to the optimum temperature for sleep.
- Make sure your room is completely dark at night to allow the release of the hormone melatonin, which helps trigger the onset of sleep.
- If blackout blinds or curtains are not in your budget, consider purchasing a blackout mask to block any ambient light you can't control.
- Avoid using screens before bed. This will reduce your exposure to blue light, which can keep you awake longer. It will also help you avoid the emotional stimulation of checking your email, scrolling through social media, or getting caught up in one more episode on Netflix.
- Enjoy a story. Reading a book can help settle instead of stimulate you. You can also listen to a bedtime story for adults. On the Calm app, celebrities read sleep stories designed to soothe you as you drift off.

In addition to avoiding food before bed, it's also wise to avoid drinking—especially when it comes to alcohol and caffeine. Caffeine is a stimulant, and it affects your body a lot like anxiety. I don't like coffee and never have, so I can't relate to the passion it ignites in others. My husband, on the other hand, can have a double espresso before bed and then go straight to sleep. You may be affected in a completely different way. Cutting back on caffeine is a personal choice, but pay attention to the effect it has on your sleep. Maybe you make the choice to stop drinking coffee by noon each day, switch to decaf, or cut it out altogether. There isn't a single right answer, because it depends on how it affects your body—but you'll never know how much it's messing with you unless you stop for a period of time.

What about alcohol? This is another personal choice, but I will say that alcohol does not produce a good quality sleep. Yes, it is a depressant—a type of sedative—but under its influence you get fragmented sleep instead of a deep, natural sleep. That's why you wake up after a night of drinking feeling less than refreshed.

Like caffeine, you should pay attention to how alcohol affects you. It's just worth being aware and noticing at what level it affects your body and your sleep. Having a glass of wine with dinner might be lovely, but finishing the bottle will not be helpful. Take note of your alcohol intake and how it affects your sleep—how many hours you get, how you feel the next day, and so on. This will inform any changes you need to make.

IDEAS FOR DAILY RELAXATION

Relaxation and sleep share a close relationship, given that one must relax in order to go to sleep, and that the body doesn't know how to relax without adequate sleep. I have chosen to separate the two, however, because there are different points throughout our day that we need a moment to relax and recharge.

One quick way to relax during the day is by practising 4-7-8 breathing. Begin by resting the tip of your tongue against the roof of your mouth, behind your top front teeth, and breathe out fully through your mouth to empty your lungs. Then breathe in through your nose for four seconds, hold your breath for seven seconds, and at a controlled pace, breathe out through your mouth for eight seconds.

The goal is to repeat this for four cycles, twice a day. It takes practice to maintain this breath cycle and feel its full effects, but stick with it. Once you've mastered four cycles, set a new goal for eight cycles. 4-7-8 breathing is useful when you can't seem to unwind enough to go to sleep, or are feeling panicky or stressed throughout the day.

Some other ideas to help you relax:

- Take a short walk and expose yourself to some natural light.
- Soak your feet in warm water mixed with epsom salts. You could also add essential oils or some bubbles—lavender is a good choice for relaxation.
- Turn down the lights, light some candles, and listen to soft music.
- Get a head massage or a facial.
- Curl up with a comfy blanket and read a good book.
- Do some light stretching.
- Connect to nature through a practice called "grounding," where you stand barefoot on either grass or sand. This actually provides you with energy as your body picks up free ions from the Earth's surface, which act as antioxidants in your system.[5]
- Practice yoga or qi gong for ten minutes. You can begin with online video tutorials. Once you've mastered them, you can do the practice on your own.
- Take a nap. This isn't lazy! It's a helpful way to recharge your mind and instantly reduce stress.
- Get crafty, or find another quiet activity: knit, paint, sketch,

5   Gaëtan Chevalier et al., "Earthing: Health Implications of Reconnecting the Human Body to the Earth's Surface Electrons," *Journal of Environmental and Public Health* 2012 (2012): 1–8. https://doi.org/10.1155/2012/291541.

play an instrument, work a puzzle, even colour in a colouring book.

· Meditate. It can be difficult to turn the "monkey mind" off, so try meditating for just three minutes at first. Find a quiet place to sit, breathe normally, and close your eyes. It's okay if your mind jumps from one thought to another. Just acknowledge them and let them go.

· Dance. With a group, a partner, or by yourself as you clean the kitchen. It gets your body moving and blood pumping.

· Watch something that makes you laugh—a romantic comedy or a quick sketch online.

· Get your hands dirty with gardening. Not only does it connect you with those earthy ions again, but there is also a very fulfilling connection between our spirits and the things we grow.

· Schedule a game night with family or friends.

· Take one drawer, or one room, and de-clutter it. This might not sound very relaxing, but you'd be surprised at how much lighter you'll feel when you bring order to your surroundings.

· Cuddle up with a pet, or volunteer at a shelter to get some quality time with a furry friend.

ARE YOU AN INFORMATION ADDICT?

We have more information hitting us at greater speeds than ever before, and it's taking a toll on our minds and bodies. Yes, knowledge is power—but there is a tipping point before the rush of information becomes too much.

FOMO, or Fear of Missing Out, is also at play here. None of us wants to be kept in the dark. By constantly checking our phones, we become addicted to being in the know, even if that means slogging through a bunch of talking heads, AI videos, and cat memes to get there.

For the sake of your physical, mental, and emotional health, it's time for a self-intervention.

- Disable some of the push notifications on your cell phone.
- Cut down on watching or reading the news. Being aware of every tragedy in the world and the horrifying images of war can negatively affect our stress levels.
- When you do watch or read the news, do not do it whilst you're eating. It can affect your digestion.

HOW TO FIND JOY IN YOUR LIFE

Let me acknowledge that finding joy and finding ways to relax have a lot of crossover. For our purposes here, I want to make some distinctions.

Relaxation amounts to taking a break and unplugging from your to-do lists and the things that stress you out. Joy, however, is more than just unplugging for a bit. True joy is a feeling that sustains us. As you search for ways to relax, you will find joy in some of those activities. The things that bring you real joy will provide a lasting sense of peace that you carry with you, even when you must plug back in.

As you try new things or revisit old activities you once loved, you may find joy in the act of reconnecting with yourself. Take the time to discover what makes you happiest, gives you peace, puts you in a meditative state, or grounds you. Not every activity in the list above will make you feel true joy, and some may even feel more like a chore. You are no worse off for discovering the latter—you tried something, it didn't work for you, and now you know this about yourself. Free yourself to explore!

If you aren't certain whether an activity brings you joy, don't stress. There's no right or wrong answer, and this is not a test. If you are involved in an activity and the time just seems to fly, that's a good indication that it brings you joy. Embrace that feeling, and try to make more time for that activity in your life. This, too, is a form of self-care.

IS EXTREME SELF-CARE SELFISH?

If you've been in the habit of people-pleasing, extreme self-care will feel a bit awkward at first. In fact, if your self-esteem has taken a beating all this time, it's going to feel downright selfish.

Read this next statement aloud:

If I don't put the focus on myself, I will have nothing left to give to others.

Self-care is not selfish. You are caring for yourself as you would your own child or another loved one. Your inner peace must be nurtured, or it will disappear under the stress of daily life. Make space to explore and experiment.

You're so used to doing that for others—but you are also worthy of the same attention.

Think about a car running on empty or that hasn't had the oil checked—eventually, it will come to a grinding halt. The problem is no longer oil or gas—the lack of either has caused additional, more expensive problems than the car would have had if it had just been properly maintained.

We, too, will break down if we do not take care of ourselves. It's not selfish—it is vital.

Don't move on from this chapter without really stopping to think, What is it I would like to have in my life that isn't happening now, and what action can I take to make that happen?

Whether it's making a call to inquire about a local singing group, remembering how much you enjoy knitting and buying some wool, or getting back on your bicycle to tootle around your neighbourhood, just take one step to move this forward.

HOW I DID IT

I opened this chapter with a difficult time from my own life. When my mother died and my husband and I were having a rough patch, I definitely didn't feel like I had time to spare to take up a new hobby. Joy seemed like a distant memory. But it was clear that I needed to make some serious changes. I decided to give myself the same tender, loving care that I was showing my little ones, starting with a new nighttime routine.

It's amazing how lonely you can feel around small children if you don't have some joy of your own. It occurred to me, however, that if I was happier, my children would be happier. By joining some local groups and meeting other mothers, I could have some grown-up conversations whilst our children played. Sometimes, we might even put together a group picnic or potluck in the park. So even though it gave me a time-out from my children, I was still present with them while creating joy for myself. What my children remember are the happy memories we made in the park, and they remember that I was there with them. The difference was that I had a built-in support system with the other mothers, who were in a similar season of life.

That doesn't mean that I never unplugged from them. Once a week, I would get a babysitter and meet a friend for a drink or lunch, just to reconnect with old friends I'd missed. I realised that I needed to nurture these relationships, because they nurtured *me*. In this difficult period of my life, I was also able to build an inner peace that was separate from my husband and our troubles. Regardless of what our future together held, I was taking care of myself.

Eventually, when we worked through our issues, I was grateful to be reunited—but I was also grateful for our time apart. The new me could not be absorbed by another person or circumstance, but I also came out of the fog with an understanding of how important relationships are to the human condition. Self-care isn't selfish, but it has its limits if you spend too much time alone. We also need to balance our alone time with connection to others.

CHAPTER 7

CONNECTING TO OTHERS

I once worked with a client named Shannon who struggled to lose weight. Lately, *everything* made Shannon cry: films, music, even sentimental television commercials. Though she got quite weepy over these things, Shannon never shared her feelings with the people around her. Crying was something she did alone.

In fact, Shannon spent a great deal of time alone.

Outside of work, Shannon lived in almost total isolation. She would come home and check emails, clean the kitchen, or find other ways to stay busy. Her husband, who was more sociable, felt ignored and started going out without her. Shannon and her husband just weren't close anymore, and Shannon seemed okay with that.

While she was alone, she ate. Instead of connecting with her husband, Shannon was using food to try to make herself feel better—but all to no avail. As she put on weight, Shannon grew ashamed of how she looked, which made her even more determined to keep her husband at arm's length.

She did not want to be touched, physically or emotionally.

Likewise, one of her old friends had been trying to get in touch with her for the last couple of years, but Shannon was so embarrassed about her appearance that she didn't feel ready to visit with her. Claiming she was "too busy," she put off her friend for months, always waiting for a day in the future when she felt better about herself.

The rest of the time, Shannon wasn't feeling present in her own life. She didn't feel like she ever fit in or belonged anywhere. She spent a good deal of time behind closed doors, numbing her emotions with food and feeling like she was living in the shadows.

"I feel like I'm waiting for my life to begin," she told me. "Once I lose the weight, I'll be able to get back to all those things I used to enjoy."

Shannon's biggest problem wasn't her weight. It was that she was totally disconnected from the people around her.

At first, Shannon was surprised that our work together wasn't solely about nutrition. A major part of the plan was to get her back out into the world. Shannon had a beautiful singing voice, so her first step was to join a local singing group. When she sang, she could watch the leader and not have to make eye contact with other people. Over time, Shannon built up her confidence in the group, particularly as she was reminded that she was a gifted singer. The ensemble was quite a sociable group, and soon Shannon was going out for a cup of tea after rehearsals or getting together with her fellow singers at a local park.

Next, Shannon made a conscious effort to connect with her husband every day. Because she felt so busy, they started with something small: they would read a couple of pages of a book. One of them would read aloud, and then they'd talk about it. It was a simple pleasure and a simple connection. From there, Shannon was inspired by her love of theatre, and they started attending every month.

Eventually, she did meet up with her old friend, and explained where she'd been and where she was headed with her weight loss. It was very emotional for her to be seen and accepted for who she is *today*—not who she was before, and not waiting for some perfect moment in the future.

Shannon realised she had to step into her new life *now*. And when she finally connected with the people around her, it made a world of difference.

WE NEED EACH OTHER

So many of our daily interactions and encounters have little to do with what is happening right in front of us. We are carrying around the baggage of our stress and insecurities, so it doesn't take much for something to set us off. For some of us, that might mean lashing out, without any thought about our tone, word choice, or whether the punishment we levy truly fits the crime. Others, like Shannon, turn inward, thinking that isolation will protect us when in fact, we are making ourselves even more vulnerable to hurt. In trying to protect herself from shame and embarrassment, Shannon actually denied herself the opportunity to share her gifts with others.

In the last chapter, I mentioned that self-care is the oxygen mask we put on ourselves. After we put on our oxygen mask, it's time to help and serve others. That is what gives us greater perspective and meaning in life. Curiosity, courtesy, and kindness are key.

Now, hanging out with our friends or attending to a friend in need is very important, and spending time with loved ones is actually a component of self-care. When I talk about connection with others in this chapter, however, I'm extending beyond those sorts of circles and including the whole human family.

Humans are made to connect. We are wired for connection, and connection is love.

When we were hunter-gatherers, we had a much better chance of surviving with others than alone. We could sleep while others kept watch for predators, or if we were injured, we could rely on the tribe for help. In turn, we also had to be there for them.

Even though we now live in this modern, digital world, we still need that connection. We still need a tribe, and connection is a primal need. If we ever had any doubt of this, being forced to live separately and in lockdown made it all crystal clear. During the COVID-19 pandemic, many people became anxious and depressed, because we require connection to others to make us feel safe.

Think back to a time when you were out of your comfort zone.

Maybe it was the first day of school, or when you started a new job, or when you attended a party where you only knew the host. All it took was someone smiling at us and talking to us in a warm, friendly manner. We no longer felt alone or ignored. We felt that connection—that inner glow of warmth makes us feel alive and totally present.

Connection can also happen when we go out of our way to do something for someone else, without expecting anything in return. Checking on an elderly neighbour, smiling at a stranger, or even doing a couple of hours a week on a helpline are small acts of kindness that serve others. But these acts also serve to heal *you* by releasing endorphins in the brain, which makes you feel happier.[6] It truly is a win-win.

THE PROBLEM WITH SOCIAL MEDIA

Though it's true that technology has given us the ability to be more connected than ever before, it doesn't provide what we yearn for. The irony of social media is that, amid its clutter, it can be more of a distraction from our loneliness than a tool to help to bring us closer together through authentic personal connection.

A 2013 study examined the feelings of envy that arise from using Facebook.[7] The study concluded that one in three people felt *worse* after visiting Facebook, especially those who weren't posting themselves, but just looking at everyone else's posts.

---

6   Peggy A. Thoits and Lyndi N. Hewitt. "Volunteer Work and Well-Being." *Journal of Health and Social Behavior* 42, no. 2 (2001): 115. https://doi.org/10.2307/3090173.

7   Hanna Krasnova et al.. "Envy on Facebook: A Hidden Threat to Users' Life Satisfaction?." paper presented at Wirtschaftsinformatik Proceedings 2013. 92. https://aisel.aisnet.org/wi2013/92.

I can understand why this is true. When we see a posted photograph of acquaintances having an intimate dinner or an amazing holiday, is that *true* connection? If anything, it can bring up feelings of inadequacy, reinforcing the feeling that we are not having the same exciting life that everyone else seems to be leading. Of course, it's a myth that everyone else's life is perfect, but it certainly can look that way on Facebook and Instagram. It's so easy to compare our insides to other people's outsides and end up feeling inadequate.

And if we do connect online via direct message or in public threads, those conversations tend to be more superficial and fleeting. This behaviour just leads to more feelings of loneliness, frustration, and possibly even anger. Although we get a little dopamine hit when our phone beeps or someone likes something that we have posted, these are poor substitutions for real connection.

I'm not saying that keeping in touch with friends and family digitally isn't wonderful and sometimes helpful, especially when we are kept physically distant by circumstances beyond our control. But actual in-person conversation is such a gift when it comes to connecting that it should be a priority whenever possible.

Now before you think I'm telling you that it's wrong to FaceTime granny, my point is that when we use this form of communication to connect *all the time*, it never quite scratches the itch. Not to mention that if you're too busy posting about life, you may not actually be living it. Instead of just relying on social media, be sure to connect to your friends and family in the real world as well.

HOW CONNECTION COMBATS OVEREATING

Many times, overeating is an attempt to compensate for the connection you are missing. But instead of making you feel better, eating often leads to the exact opposite of connection: isolation.

I remember what it was like, going out with friends and eating normally in public but then coming home to eat more at home—even though I was already completely full. This overeating occurred behind closed doors, where I could hide the emptiness and sadness I believed could never be shared.

Connecting to other people counteracts these impulses. It's a great way to fill up your soul instead of attempting to do that with food. There will never be enough food to fill that void. Overeating is hurting you. The excess food isn't just bad for your body. It also makes you feel bad about yourself, which keeps you isolated and works against connecting to others.

And isn't connection what we are truly longing for, deep down? Real connection works against irritability and helps us feel really good about ourselves on a deep, spiritual level. As your self-esteem grows, you begin to fill that void inside of you and discover that:

- You do belong.
- You are good enough.
- You are worthy of joy.

When we feel lonely and we just need something, *anything* to make us feel better, we think food is a solution. It is not. It can never be enough. Our loneliness can reveal itself as irritability or anger. It's the perfect storm that makes us turn to a packet of chocolate biscuits, alone and ashamed.

The antidote is connection. The love and fulfilment you get from seeing a dear friend is immeasurable and priceless. Connection doesn't just happen through laughter, either. In fact, some of the most precious connections occur when someone is going through a very difficult time. Being heard, listened to, and noticed can make such a difference in a person's life, whether they are giving or receiving the attention. Food becomes less of a priority, because it cannot love and care for you the way a friend can. And no matter how much we "love" crisps and biscuits, we cannot possibly love them as much as we do a real friend.

HOW TO BUILD STRONGER CONNECTIONS TO OTHERS

A truly amazing thing occurs when we genuinely connect with someone—it reciprocates. I want to emphasise the word *genuinely* here, because I do not believe the cliché that we get what we give. In fact, part of the reason we overeat is because we give and have not received, so when I talk about genuine connection, that's when it becomes reciprocal: We give *and* we receive from another human being. Not necessarily equal amounts at equal times, but neither party feels overburdened or desperate.

When we genuinely connect, we learn more about ourselves, because we are fully present.

The more self-aware we become, the more we understand what we truly need. When we are rooted in self-awareness, we have more compassion and love for ourselves—which, in turn, positions us to build better connections with others.

The following ideas should serve as a springboard to connect more deeply with others:

- Commit to being present at meal times—no screens at the table. This will help you be more mindful about both your relationships and the food you eat.
- When you are with a friend or family member, focus on the quality of your time together. Make a point to engage them with questions, take an interest in their day, and make a mental note of anything you might want to follow up with at a later time.
- Every few months, make it a priority to visit a family member or loved one who lives in another town.
- Go see a live show—music, theatre, or comedy—and make some memories with friends.
- Support your community. In my village, there's a volunteer opportunity to visit someone who is housebound or just lonely. You might also volunteer at a local primary school or library to read with children. Find a way to help that matches your interests.
- Learn a new skill or rekindle a childhood hobby. This will often lead to meeting new people with similar passions.
- Have a date night with your spouse.

Connection doesn't have to be made in grand gestures. It could be as simple as noticing someone at a gathering and making them feel welcome. You know what it feels like to walk into a room and feel self-conscious, so make an effort to ensure it doesn't happen to someone else. Phone a friend, rake leaves for an elderly neighbour, and think of ways to keep your mind occupied and hands busy besides reaching for food. Look for small opportunities to connect with others, whether for a moment, a season, or a lifetime—they can happen at the most unexpected of times.

In my younger days, I had a Saturday job showing people around properties for the local estate agents. One day, I was showing someone a house, and when we went to leave, we discovered that the lock was faulty. We couldn't get out! When I phoned for help, everybody in the office was busy for the next couple of hours. It was a lovely afternoon, though, so I sat with this young man and chatted. He was younger than me by several years. During our conversation, he opened his heart and told me how his brother had recently died from a drug overdose. It was possibly intentional, possibly not. But as he said, he would never be able to ask him, and his parents would never really know. I couldn't take his pain away, but I could sit with him and listen.

Sometimes, it's easier to tell a stranger what is going on with you. All this young man really needed was for someone to listen. When one of the agents finally showed up to let us out, he was quite surprised that, before the young man said goodbye, we had a long, heartfelt hug.

We had connected, and it meant something.

When we shift our focus away from ourselves onto others and really want to support them, it reminds us that we have meaning and worth—and that we can make a difference.

WE ARE A SOCIAL SPECIES

Our evolutionary design indicates that connection was an important part of our survival, since it improved our chances of collecting food, building shelter, and staying safe. We all know the catastrophic effects for a baby who may have been given sufficient food and milk but not cuddles, love, and face-to-face connection. The same is true for isolated adults.

Interpersonal connection and love are essential to every aspect of our health and well-being. As we go through our lives, connection helps us regulate our emotions, leads to higher self-esteem, and lessens the loneliness that makes us seek more food than we actually need.

We all get the concept that people can fall in love with each other, but you can also fall in love with the moment, which refreshes and revitalises you, making you feel connected all over again. Perhaps you are learning something new together, or taking a trip to a destination neither of you has visited before. Or maybe you are just reflecting—in gratitude—on a wonderful memory you share. In any instance, you are connecting not only to the other person or the moment, but to life itself. You feel present, you feel like an active participant in your own life. It's a great way to fill up on what you really need.

TURN YOUR LIFE AROUND, ONE CONNECTION POINT AT A TIME

As Shannon experienced the joy of actively living her life, that life began to change. Food was calling her less, and instead she was filling up with connection, joy, and friendship. As the weight came off and Shannon's wardrobe changed, so did the way she expressed herself. When she was out shopping, for example, she found herself chatting to people instead of her usual head-down-and-get-on-with-it stance. These moments of connection helped her open up to the world around her, and she was able to both laugh and cry in our sessions.

As others began to notice her weight loss, Shannon still found it excruciating when they complimented her appearance. She initially responded with something like, "Oh, I've got so much more to lose," or "I have such a long way to go," and other statements that diminished her achievement. In time, however, she learned to look at them with a smile and say, "Thank you." Making connections, forming relationships, and enjoying new friends was rewarding and kept her going. And in time, Shannon reached her goal weight.

There is a deep, profound healing that takes place when you give and receive love. Just as a baby and mother communicate their love through their eyes, that sacred connection is something we need beyond infancy. We can still do that for ourselves, and for others. Connection is a type of love we all still need to experience.

Once we ourselves are on solid footing, we are in a better position to be there for other people. The beautiful thing about that is the new pathways to healing that can open up, sometimes radiating outwards in a ripple effect of good feeling, and sometimes healing and resolving matters from the past. As we build stronger connections with others, we will build our emotional reserves to put all that we have learned about awareness, acceptance, and action into practice to overcome our most difficult personal challenges.

PART TWO

THE PRACTICE

In Part One, we looked at all the ways in which your thoughts and emotions are running the show when it comes to over-eating. Truly, it is not about the food—it's about your feelings and the way you choose to deal with them when they become uncomfortable. You have the power to break out of the fear-eat-regret cycle of eating by pressing the pause button to see what's really going on in the moment you reach for food. You have all the tools to give yourself proper self-care and make better choices when you are sad, stressed, angry, or hurt.

Knowledge is power, but none of this is easy or automatic. When you have a difficult relationship with food, putting the tenets of **awareness, acceptance,** and **action** into practice takes time. To help you get started on the journey, we will now look at how to put these ideas into practice to help you overcome several specific emotional challenges that often keep people returning to food for comfort—even when they desperately want to stop overeating.

CHAPTER 8

LOVING LITTLE YOU

If you recall the mini-fridge incident from Chapter 1, you may have caught a hint that my relationship with my stepfather wasn't exactly warm and loving. This does not mean he was to blame for my overeating, but rather that our family situation was a perfect environment for it to thrive in.

He got together with my mother when I was seven and my brother was twelve. It was clear from the outset that two children were not part of his plan, and our very presence was unpleasant for him. We were either ignored or criticised, the latter always accompanied by his enraged temper. We learned soon enough to keep a low profile.

That's when eating became my salvation. As a child, I wasn't equipped to understand what was going on, so I sought solace instead of solutions. It would be decades before I realised this childhood pattern of behaviour set me on a path of continued self-punishment with food, long after I had grown up and left home for good.

Once, when I was around age ten or eleven, I arrived home from school just as I did every day. On that day, my stepfather just started screaming at me, and I didn't know what I had done. By then, my antenna was always up, checking the climate of the house, so to speak. I was excellent at feeling out whether they had just had an argument or whether it was a calm day. But that day, I didn't have any warning. He just came at me, screaming for no reason.

I ran to my room sobbing, and my mother walked in. "It's not your fault," she tried to reassure me. "You've done nothing wrong. He wants to get at me. He is just shouting at you to upset me."

That made no sense to me then, and it doesn't make sense to me now. The only difference is that I've had decades of life experience and know the toll that adult stress and disappointment can take on a child.

As an adult, I now know that eating doesn't help the situation at all. But as a child, eating was all I had. It was one of the only things in my life that I had any control over, and I didn't know there were other options to comfort myself.

THE IMPACT OF DYSFUNCTION

We are born whole. None of us entered this world to harm and punish ourselves with food. We did not leave the womb hating ourselves and our bodies.

If a child's spirit is nurtured and allowed to flourish, then that child learns to trust life. Sometimes, however, trust is whittled away early on, and as children we learn survival tactics that don't take us into a healthy adulthood. Our fear, anger, and despair stem from being unable to express or even understand these feelings—to the point where we may have learned not to have feelings in the first place.

You may look like a responsible grownup, but Little You is running the show and still throwing toys out of the pram. There remains a need to be seen and heard, regardless of our age.

I want to pause here, before we go any further. It's easy to fall into blame and self-pity when we realise that many of our issues stem from childhood. What I would caution before laying blame is that these are learned or acquired behaviours.

Just as you are not to be blamed for things that happened in your childhood, the blame also doesn't lie with your parents. They may have gone through similar difficulties in their upbringing and were just doing their best, having been faultily equipped themselves. Whether your childhood dysfunction included adults who raged at, manipulated, or neglected you, remember that it's highly probable that they acted out because they experienced similar patterns. Their own dysfunction is more than likely due to Little Them not receiving the love, compassion, and cherishing *they* deserved.

For me, it didn't matter how many diets I went on or how much weight I lost—at my core, I didn't feel good about myself, and this feeling began in childhood. I didn't feel worthy or deserving, so the food would call and the weight would pile back on.

We have to recover that childlike hope, wonder, and peace that were taken away. As adults, we can stop the cycle of dysfunction.

It's time to heal Little You.

AWARENESS: WHEN OLD FEELINGS BUBBLE UP

Have you ever squeezed a half-inflated balloon? It shifts and bubbles out between your fingers in odd ways. The balloon is still there. It's still half-inflated, and it will find little escape hatches until it finally pops.

When we try to push down our uncomfortable feelings, the same thing happens. We *think* we are hiding them or making them disappear, but they manage to escape via our reactions until *we* finally pop.

The first step to healing is always awareness. Right now, you are not equipped to heal Little You, perhaps because you're not sure what exactly is broken. Just like my eight-year-old self eating all the nuts and raisins that day, you may not yet know the specifics—you just know something is wrong.

So let's deepen that awareness. When you think back to your childhood, did you have needs that weren't met? If you're not sure or don't trust your perspective, ask yourself the following questions, thinking through how you react now as an adult:

- Does the world feel like an unsafe place to be?
- Do you feel an underlying sense that something is lacking in your life?
- Do you feel you can't ask others to meet your needs?
- Do you hide what is really going on with you and put on a happy front for others?

If you answered *yes* to any of these, it's time to open the door of compassion to Little You. Once Little You walks through it, you can understand why you react the way you do in certain situations and put a stop to the continual self-blame and feelings of failure.

No matter what you were missing in your childhood, I want you to know that reaching for food is a normal way for a child to deal with pain and longing. Babies cry when they are hungry, after all, and food soothes—at first. It's a natural, honest reaction to feed a baby as a means of comfort. Then as children, food becomes a very handy tool, because we may have thought that something that *tastes* good might make us *feel* good.

This reaction was a normal response to an unhealthy situation. Left unchecked, however, we eventually don't even care if it tastes good. We just want to feel good or, at the very least, keep the uncomfortable feelings away. By then, we've entered the fear-eat-regret cycle.

Remember my story from Chapter 1 about being at a friend's house and eating all the nuts and raisins that had been put out for guests? I kept putting my little hand into the jar, eating more and more, until I felt uncomfortable. I didn't know about diets then, but I remember clearly thinking that what I had done was wrong. I wasn't overweight at that age, but the unhealthy relationship with my emotions and with eating had already begun.

If for any reason as children our world didn't feel safe, we learned behaviours to try and cope with them. These coping mechanisms didn't do us any favours. The more we run from our feelings, the more they pursue us. They will catch up with you and trip you every time. And down you go, face-down, into pie, cake, crisps, and so on.

Whether your overeating started in childhood or not, we often don't like to express our needs in case they're not met. In many respects, it's easier to push them down and ignore the uncomfortable feelings than it is to be open and vulnerable. It gives you a sense of control because at least you're the one doing the pushing—except you always feel worse afterwards.

Does this sound like you? Do you have unresolved pain from your childhood that you're trying to soothe? Or did you learn to comfort yourself with food and have kept the habit going into adulthood? These are difficult questions, and it will take time to sit with them and get at the truth of what's going on inside of you. But becoming aware of your unmet needs is the crucial first step in taking care of Little You.

ACCEPTANCE: NOT EVERY FEELING REQUIRES A REACTION

Once we have acknowledged our needs, what we really need to do is learn to have feelings without having to react to them. We need to create a temporary space for the uncomfortable feelings, so we can sit with them without judgement. Through acceptance, we will give those feelings permission to move on instead of pushing them down and reaching for food as a comfort.

This pause to feel and accept also creates space for choices instead of obsessions and compulsions. Compulsions take away our ability to say *no* and instead bring huge feelings of shame and failure. Choices, however, give us a bit of time to weigh the possible outcomes. We respond instead of react.

There is a line that separates awareness and acceptance, and I will use my own experience to demonstrate how that works. From a very young age, my mother was always telling me and my brother that we would leave my stepfather and start a new life on our own. This was music to my ears, and I would be elated at the prospect of a new beginning, only to feel completely let down and forgotten when it never happened. Worse yet, no one ever explained why or confirmed it wasn't going to happen, so I held on to the constant hope without any resolution.

As an adult, if someone said to me that something was going to happen, and then it didn't, *boom!* I went straight back to the food, completely unaware that I was reacting to disappointment and stuffing my emotions down just as I did when I was little. Disappointment after disappointment, I would simply shut down, reminding myself that they didn't care, I wasn't lovable, and I didn't deserve whatever they had promised anyway. That was my pattern.

It didn't occur to me that sometimes things just don't work out the way someone plans, even when they sincerely believe it when they tell you that it will. Once I was aware of this pattern of my own behaviour, I could accept that I could be disappointed without the bottom falling out. I didn't have to be the little girl who felt unnoticed and uncared for—that's who was running the show when the fridge door opened. Now that I have developed and used the tools to choose a different response, I can say that doesn't happen anymore.

If you react strongly to an interaction with someone for no apparent reason, take a moment to consider if something has triggered a response or memory from your childhood. While it's important to take a *glance* back to childhood to find out where the reaction is rooted, it is equally important not to get lost in it. The glance should be helpful in understanding ourselves and how these feelings affect our current behaviour. When you begin to notice when you enter a reactive state, you can pause, reflect, and move towards acceptance. This is the way to stop reacting and learn to respond differently.

We need to understand and accept before we can take action to stop.

ACTION: BREAK OLD PATTERNS AND EMBRACE LOVING BEHAVIOURS

Once I worked with a client—we'll call her Melanie—who told me that when she was a child, her mother was constantly criticising other people. If a friend came over for a visit, the moment they left, her mother would start complaining about how much food they had eaten, how ungrateful they were, and how rude they had been. As a child, Melanie was confused because she always thought everyone had had a lovely time, and didn't understand where it had all gone so wrong. As a result, whenever Melanie went to a friend's house, she was always really careful about how much food she would eat, so as not to be criticised in the same way. Ultimately, Melanie didn't enjoy going over to friends' houses because of the constant worrying over how they would talk about her once she left.

When she arrived back home hungry after one of these visits, Melanie would stuff herself with food. She was starving! But she was also trying to counteract the emotions of what mean gossip could possibly be going on behind her back. In her world, that's what happened when someone left the room, so it stood to reason—albeit a child's reason—that's what happened when *she* left a room too. She wanted to give them as little as possible to gossip about.

When something like that occurs early in life, it's so ingrained in us that it becomes part of our default system. As children, it's normalised, and therefore carried into our adulthood. We no longer think about it or question it. We just think that's the way things are. In Melanie's case, she could not trust that if she left a room, she would not be gossiped about, because her mother routinely criticised people the moment they were out of earshot. This may seem ridiculous, but that had been ingrained into her as a very young child. It never occurred to her to question her mother's behaviour or to think that perhaps that's not how the rest of the world operates.

When you become aware that some of your strong reactions come from childhood triggers and you accept that they might have been normalised when they shouldn't have been, you can take action to change your own behaviour. Recognise that this does *not* mean that everyone around you will change theirs; you have no control over that. If you have someone in your life who behaves the way Melanie's mother did, understand that they will likely continue to criticise everyone who leaves the room. You can be hopeful that in time, that might change, but don't count on it. Make your own change so that your responses and behaviour are not contingent on theirs.

Start by taking notice of any recurring patterns you're experiencing with certain people or situations. If your reaction is strong and upsetting, if you feel angry or let down time and again, the hurts of your past and the hurts of your present are likely converging.

Remember, this is not about them, what they're doing, or what they did. This is about your own behaviour. When you can see your pattern and what triggered it, you are empowered to press the pause button and respond instead of react. Obviously, you can't change your past, but what you can change is the extent of its influence on your present. Accept this, and resolve to change course moving forward. Instead of blaming yourself for failure, be gentle with yourself. The action steps may be painful at times, because you are unlearning things that have been buried deep within you for most of your life. Whether it was a belief that was inflicted on you, as in my own experience, or your own child-mind internalised a modelled behaviour, as in Melanie's experience, you are untangling a large, tight, twisted knot of thinking. This will take time, so be compassionate and forgiving when Little You makes a mistake.

RE-PARENTING LITTLE YOU

The action steps you will take are, in a sense, re-parenting the child whose needs were not met. Think of Adult You parenting Little You to provide what Little You did not receive the first time around.

Find a childhood photograph of yourself—ideally, at around two to five years old. Put it on the wall, in a frame, or even on the refrigerator door. Put it somewhere you'll see it often, as a reminder that this child is getting another opportunity to be nurtured and cared for in healthy ways.

Really study that precious Little You, shiny-eyed and full of hope. A precious gem deserving so much care, attention, and love. What would you say to them? What do you wish for them? If it helps, speak aloud to that child how you intend to meet their needs, and remain true to your word. Little You needs to trust you in ways they could not trust other adults.

When you engage in negative self-talk, whether it's berating yourself for overeating or judging yourself for not being good enough, not achieving enough, or not being the right size, make a point to go look at that photo. You are saying these mean things to that child. In fact, the voice you hear may not be your own—it may be that of a parent, a teacher, or some other adult—and you are putting those hurtful words into their mouths to speak to Little You. It's time for Adult You to step in and make good on your promise to nurture and protect yourself.

What we are doing here is dissecting our feelings—not just where they originated, but how they were cultivated, how they shaped your perspective, and whether the triggers are valid. Let's be clear: your feelings were and are valid, but they are a reaction to something that may not have been valid. Instead of eating your feelings as you may have done for many years, recognise that all those years of overeating have been an attempt to numb and quiet your inner child's pain.

You are ready to deal with the pain of these emotions. You don't have to act on them by reaching for food. Press the pause button and, as you work through these feelings, consider the source, the weight, the influence, and the trigger, and try to look at them as objectively as possible.

Ask Little You the following questions:

- What did precious Little You need when you were small?
- What do you need right now, at this moment?

Your old way of reacting isn't working, so just take the risk and try this, even if it seems awkward. Go look at the photo. Perhaps you will find it easier to ask the child in the photo, because you'll think that they are more deserving and vulnerable of your care and attention. That child wants and deserves to experience life with joy and love.

By the time we hit adolescence, we learn to pretend to give a different impression than what's really going on underneath the surface with us. We learn to wear a mask and hide behind it. As adults, the masks become more widespread: we hide behind our competent image, a job, or even a car. Behind closed doors, we use eating to try and deal with what's really going on with us.

It's time to offer yourself the love that you would offer a small, innocent child. The parts you missed out on as a child—the parts that illuminated all the possibilities and choices that will give you freedom. As you work through this process, it is okay to feel upset, angry, or sad about whatever you didn't have or missed out on—you now know how to give the feelings a temporary space, acknowledge them without judgement, then let them move on. Recall the extreme self-care we talked about, and put those tools into practice to help you through the difficult waves of feeling.

Tell Little You that they did the only thing they knew to do. When we were young, we didn't know about these possibilities and choices, but now we are learning that we have options. If we make a different choice, we become more aware and responsible, and that leads to great freedom in our lives. Explain to Little You that they have punished themselves with food because somewhere along the way, they were convinced that they were not worthy of anything. Gently tell Little You that's not true—Little You is worthy and deserving of freedom.

As you stop blaming yourself and see that you were just reacting in order to cope in a painful world, you can begin to have different, healthier beliefs.

FROM PHOTO TO MIRROR

Now I want you to transition from the photo of adorable Little You to the mirror of Adult You. They are both the same person, and they are both worthy and deserving of love, fulfilment, and freedom.

Motivational author Louise Hay gave a talk back in 1987 where she provided a list of "mirror statements" that align with our intentions here. So go look at yourself in the mirror. Look deep into your eyes with pure compassion, and say the following:

- *I love you.*
- *You are safe with me.*
- *What can I do today to make you happy?*
- *I will stop punishing you.*
- *I will treat you kindly.*
- *I will listen to you and be considerate of you.*
- *I will nurture you.*
- *It's time now to be healed.*

- *I am loved.*
- *I am love.*
- *I am safe.*

If you need to tape the childhood photo to your mirror to remind you that you are one and the same and both deserving of compassion, then by all means, do so. Let that serve as the guiding point of how to treat yourself with care and concern.

As children, we relied on others for love, nourishment, and care. Some of us received more than others, but as adults, we still need that love and care today. We are not dependent on others, be it parents or anyone else, to provide what we need. We can be the ones responsible for taking care of ourselves.

You have your own back now. When you reach for the food, imagine how much love Little You deserves. That's how much care, attention, and nurturing you deserve right at that crucial moment. It's not always easy, but if you manage to do it just once, you can do it again. This small but significant moment can open the door that leads to great peace. It's a powerful way of loving ourselves at a very deep level.

WE'VE TRAVELLED DIFFERENT PATHS TO GET HERE

Some of you may be able to trace your childhood trigger to a single, trajectory-changing moment that had you pacifying yourself with food. Others, like me, may have no single defining moment, just a number of confusing experiences that were never explained or re-addressed when they didn't work out. How you arrived where you are today isn't nearly as important as where you are headed.

We can break the cycle of repeated dieting and reaction when we work on our underlying conditions. It's important to recognise their origins not to lay blame on any one person or situation, but to understand that perspectives may have been skewed, circumstances may have been normalised, and our internalised beliefs were built on faulty foundations. Once I saw my own childhood eating triggers a bit more clearly, I was free to make other choices.

That's when the weight started coming off—and stayed off for good.

Once we are aware of how our childhood made an impact on our eating habits, and we accept that it may not have been right or fair, we can take proper actions to right the ship. This is a difficult process and it will take time, because it isn't just about food.

At some point, you will arrive at a painful threshold, and you'll want to retreat. This is the catalyst that will change your relationship with food. This is also where self-care and being your own best friend, parent, and caretaker will help you to cross it and keep going. This is just the beginning of the journey.

The journey continues as you learn to dig deeper into your emotions and feel all of your feelings—even the most difficult ones.

CHAPTER 9

FEEL YOUR FEELINGS

At my mother's funeral, I felt absolutely nothing. I was completely numb. My lack of emotion was confusing, but also kind of relieved me, as I thought maybe I had managed to sidestep the grief I was expecting to feel. In fact, I thought I was handling things rather well, considering how much I loved her and how close we were.

It would be many months later that the pain hit me, unexpectedly and viscerally. The grief was overwhelming. It shook my body, and yet, there was a sweetness to it. I made space to feel it instead of fighting it and let it wash over me. Once it was released, I felt a sense of calm and acceptance.

Now, this doesn't mean I had one good cry and it was done. Once the grief arrived, I lost count of how many times it would hit. I could feel its arrival in my body, rising up from the gut and crashing over me. From there, without prompting, I was in uncontrollable tears. This was not a movie-star cry with a few delicate tears dabbing my cheeks. No, this was full-on, proper sobbing and wailing. It came in waves, arriving then receding like the tide. Each time, I knew to let it wash over me, knowing that if I allowed myself to feel it, in time it would diminish. In many respects, I encouraged the waves to come. I wanted to experience my grief fully, so as not to retain any of it and have it manifest into destructive habits and behaviours—including overeating.

THE CLEANSING POWER OF A GOOD CRY

By now you know what a terrible weapon food makes. Ultimately, it cannot help us win the battle we seem to have with our feelings. When we realise that we should not actually be at war with our feelings, the question to ask is: *What were we fighting them for?*

You cannot numb your feelings with food, nor will they go away—they will persist, more aggressively, until you allow yourself to feel them. But your feelings only want to reside with you temporarily. There is no need to run from them, push them away, or try to escape them. They are just passing through, and it is okay to cry when they do.

As children, we are often told not to cry. We are praised as strong or good for not causing any fuss. Not crying equaled strength. As adults, then, we praise others for holding it together during adversity. Why do we think that suppressing emotions is a way to show our strength? What is wrong with human beings having feelings?

When you suppress an emotion, it usually means you are pushing aside some sort of learning opportunity and choosing instead to wear a mask that will be acceptable to the external world. This is tied to the fear-eat-regret cycle, because we often fear what would happen if the emotions are expressed.

If everything around you is falling apart, this constant running from your emotions comes with a cost. For people like us, the consequence is that we reach for food. We are trying to control our feelings when in fact, they will run the show with every mindless trip to the kitchen. Then of course, you end up feeling worse after eating. If you're anything like me, you've had this song on repeat for a long time. It's the old cycle of fear-eat-regret, but it's time to press the pause button.

We repeat these patterns without even realising, taking occasional detours to go on a diet or to try a new exercise plan, only to circle back around and do it all again. It's natural to want to avoid uncomfortable feelings, and sometimes it can actually be easier to hold it together instead of embracing difficult emotions.

But the easy choice isn't always the healthiest. So let's walk through the steps of awareness, acceptance, and action to do the difficult but rewarding work of *feeling our feelings*—no matter how impossibly challenging they seem to be.

AWARENESS: IDENTIFYING YOUR EMOTIONS

Food can be so comforting, but its comfort is more temporary than any one of your uncomfortable emotions. In a moment, the comfort food brings is gone, and you are right back on the battle lines with your feelings.

Emotions are valuable. They deserve your attention, and they need to be expressed. Think about that word: *expressed*. Your feelings literally need to get out, to be expressed from your body and soul, just as you squeeze a lemon to express its sour juice, or as you wring out a sponge to release the water from its pores.

You may have been raised to believe, on some level, that emotions are bad and must be ignored and suppressed. Thinking back to our balloon-squeezing analogy from the previous chapter, we were either taught or conditioned to squeeze our emotions down into a manageable package, yet they would still pop out in inconvenient ways, no matter how hard we tried to rein them in.

Self-control is a form of emotional management, not suppression. There is a difference. Managing your emotions means allowing yourself to feel them and controlling your *reaction* to them so you do not harm yourself with food or others with poor choices. This is quite different from suppressing your feelings and hoping that they go away. As you learn the distinction, remember to be compassionate, kind, and understanding with yourself.

A good cry acknowledges the feelings that have arrived and cleanses your soul. Let the tears clean out all that has been residing in you. What a relief it is to just let those feelings out and to no longer be under their influence!

Difficult thoughts and feelings happen for everyone. It's just part of life. We can't possibly know the value of those feelings without first identifying and acknowledging them.

For many of us, identifying emotions may seem like untangling a knot, but even if we get that far, our emotions are not necessarily linear. We might not be aware of the full spectrum of our emotions. We go from rage to happiness without being aware of all the finer points or degrees of whatever we are feeling. For example, we often confuse anger with fear or sadness.

Did you know we can have a biochemical reaction along with an emotional reaction? This is quite helpful when we are trying to simply identify what we are feeling. The next time you are hit with a wave of emotion, pause and take a body scan. Now answer the following:

· Has your breathing rate increased?
· Can you feel butterflies in your stomach?
· Is your heart racing?
· Is your body tense?
· Are you frowning?
· Has your jaw or face tightened?

Once you start to connect your physical reaction to specific emotions, you can begin to identify what fear feels like, what anger feels like, what sadness feels like, and so on. Most of us can name the big feelings of happy, sad, or angry, but getting into the details is trickier. Take a look at the feeling wheel below to see just how vast the range of human emotion is.

THE EMOTION WHEEL

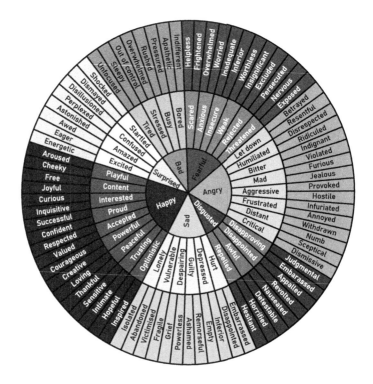

The next time you find yourself dealing with a strong emotion, use the emotion wheel to help you name it. Start at the centre and choose the feeling from that tier that most closely matches your experience. From there, explore outwards into the next ring to fine-tune your ability to name that emotion. For example, if you feel sad, is it that you are lonely, hurt, or depressed? Continue moving outwards to get more specific. When we know exactly what we are feeling, we can call it by name. This may feel a bit wobbly at first, so be kind to yourself. Use the extreme self-care tools you have acquired and extend some grace as you learn. It takes practice to become fluent in this skill.

ACCEPTANCE: TIME TO MOVE ON

When we know exactly what we are feeling, we can move forward into acceptance. When we identify our emotions and say aloud, "I feel _____," this automatically puts our feelings in proper, manageable perspective. You have called the emotion by its name—sadness, frustration, anger, hurt—whatever it may be. It's no longer a looming shadow that haunts you. You have called it out for what it is.

Now you can accept that emotion. So sit with it for a moment. Remind yourself that it's okay to feel this specific emotion. You are allowed to feel it, and even to welcome its presence. Let it dwell with you as long as it needs to—don't try and hasten its departure. If you need to cry, cry. If you need to feel angry or helpless or even laugh out loud, do it. Let the feeling be what it is, and allow your body to respond naturally.

You should not push a feeling away, nor should you cling to it in stubbornness or because it's become too familiar. Feelings are temporary—when it's time to release it, let it go. Acceptance opens the door for the feeling to enter, but also for it to leave again when it is ready to go.

ACTION: HEALTHY WAYS TO MANAGE EMOTIONS

We have identified the emotions, and welcomed them by name. Managing them also takes practice, but it is necessary. Otherwise, we are simply finding more creative ways to suppress them while they linger and magnify their presence in our lives.

When we talk about managing emotions, part of the "action" is learning that not every emotion you experience requires a reaction. We have spent time in earlier chapters learning the difference between reaction and response. Managing negative and uncomfortable emotions is the *response*: you are not lashing out, nor are you eating to shove the feelings down. Your response is measured, present, and calm. You are choosing to sit with the emotion and process it instead of acting out on it.

Earlier in the chapter, we talked about the biochemical, physical response that takes place when we are hit with something that triggers uncomfortable emotions. In the interest of survival, our bodies don't know the difference between a critical mother or a bear attack; the body, at the cellular level, just knows to get into fight-or-flight mode. I had suggested a total body scan as part of identifying the emotion, but now I want us to revisit this and go deeper. The actions you will take to manage your feelings will work in tandem with the body scan.

As you scan, take note of any physical changes taking place. We have identified some possibilities, like quickened breathing, racing heart, and muscular tension, but this is about *you*. Make note of any and all physical changes you feel in your body, not just the ones mentioned in this chapter.

Now it's time to apply some action. The following tools and exercises will help you learn how to manage the negative emotions that each of us deal with:

- Practice the 4-7-8 breathing you learned in Chapter 6.
- Tense and release different parts of your body. As you relax each part, focus on exhaling and sinking into the emotion you're experiencing in your body.

- Welcome what you are experiencing and feeling at this moment as an opportunity to learn.
- Say aloud: "I feel _____. I am allowed to feel _____. And I welcome _____ for as long as it needs to stay, but not a moment longer than that."
- If you're struggling to identify the emotion, try whittling it down. Take some time to think about what is *really* upsetting you beyond the event that set you off, and say it out loud. For example: "I am angry, because I am sad, because I am hurt, because _____." Saying this out loud is a good way to begin pulling those deeply rooted feelings to the surface. Don't try to suppress them, just let them come up.
- Take a few minutes to sit with your feelings. You can ask yourself, *Where is this feeling in my body?*
- If you need to move your body, do that, too. Stretch, go for a walk, or perhaps punch a pillow.
- When you're ready, let go by saying, *I let go of my need to control and eat. I accept this emotion as it is.*
- Now ask yourself, *What do I really need right now instead of food?*

Don't worry if you find this difficult—you are stepping outside your comfort zone and overcoming the training you may have had as a child to push down these feelings. Take a moment now to acknowledge your courage and willingness to try. If the tears come, let them flow. Remember, crying can feel so cathartic; it actually releases oxytocin and endorphins, those feel-good hormones that help heal both physical and emotional pain. Emotional tears flush stress, hormones, and other toxins out of your system, so embrace them. Your body wants you to release these emotions and process them.

It's so important to have love and compassion for yourself while you're doing this important work. Keep letting those waves of emotions roll over you. They will roll out and leave room for something else. Now you've made a space to step out of the same destructive pattern and make a different choice for yourself.

Finally, it's a good idea to make a list of immediate actions to support you when you're going through an emotional time. This work may seem very logical and doable in theory, but when a strong emotion hits, it's helpful to have a reminder of what to do. There may be particular actions in this book that resonate with you more than others, so keep the list handy before you actually need it. In time, these actions will practically become a reflex. The key is to check in with yourself and ask, *What do I need now to move forward?*

CATCH AND RELEASE

We need to become comfortable sitting with uncomfortable emotions. They need to be caught before they morph and magnify into something they are not supposed to be. Once we have identified those feelings, we need to embrace them. We do this to understand that feelings are temporary, and we need only embrace them for a short period of time. We don't have to react to every emotion.

The feelings will pass, and we need to be in tune enough with ourselves to know when it's time to release them. Feelings are not forever. If you can name the emotion that you are going through, ask it, *What is this feeling making me want to do right now? What is it really about?* You are allowed to feel angry, but you don't have to act out in a self-destructive way or in a way that hurts another person—even if that person has hurt *you*.

I have already told you about the rollercoaster ride our family was on with regard to my mother and stepfather, and that it took me several months before the grief over her death washed over me. As the tears flowed, the most bizarre but beautiful thing happened: all these good memories with her flooded into my mind and heart, like a short film reel of precious moments I had with her. I was able to relive so many deeply buried memories of good times we had together. It was lovely, and it brought me great joy. I realised it was only because I was willing to walk *through* my pain that I was able to arrive at a place where I felt safe and open. The spectrum of emotions that followed unlocked some surprising revelations about myself, about her, and about life in general.

You cannot live a full life without emotions. When we push our feelings away through knee-jerk reactions, we are also pushing life itself away. Pause long enough to make a wiser choice. Instead of acting on impulse and spiralling out of control, hit your pause button and sit with the feelings. Sift down to what you are *really* feeling, and pinpoint why you're feeling this way. They are not the giant, looming shadows that you fear. They are not to be pushed away so that they come back stronger. Emotions are much, much more manageable than that.

When you get right down to it, you get to choose your own adventure in life—and it's a choice between love or fear. Trust yourself enough to choose love.

CHAPTER 10

SHAME

Remember Melanie's story from Chapter 8? Her mother was constantly criticising others, and Melanie's relationship with her was challenging at best. As a teenager, Melanie began putting on weight, and her mother never ceased making comments about it. Melanie felt as though she didn't live up to her mother's expectations in any way, and as a typical teen, Melanie began acting out. For example, if her mother commented that what she was eating was fattening and that she really shouldn't be putting on any more weight, Melanie would eat more of it, just for spite.

As an adult with children of her own, Melanie still had an uneasy relationship with her mother. Melanie felt constantly criticised for every life choice, from meal prep to home decor. She managed to keep her rebellious teenage spirit under control, at least in front of her mother. For example, she might eat a normal lunch while visiting Mum, then stuff herself with anything she could find once she arrived home. It was the constant, gnawing resentment Melanie felt towards her mother that kept her on edge. Though she always hoped for a loving, understanding mum, Melanie had a blaming, dismissive one instead.

Well into adulthood, Melanie still felt there was something wrong with her. She never felt she lived up to her mother's expectations. Never once did her mother compliment her or allow that perhaps she was doing some things right. What Melanie heard was that she was never quite good enough, never made the right decisions—even her parenting was lacklustre. More often than not, if one of Melanie's children acted out, her mother would make remarks like, "I never let *you* get away with *that*."

Now it's possible that Melanie's mother meant those off-handed comments as helpful suggestions, but some of us just can't roll with all the little digs. They eat away at our self-confidence. When we are subjected to constant criticism at a young age, it seeps into the DNA. Maybe it starts with food, or our marks in school, or perhaps we aren't as outgoing as someone thought we should be. Whatever the initial criticism was, it compounds from there until we feel we can never measure up to any standard.

In Melanie's case, it all started with food. Her mother made comments like:

"Oh, you really shouldn't have any more of that."

"You don't want to be putting on any more weight, do you?"

"Haven't you already had enough?"

By the time she came to see me, Melanie had got to the point where she no longer recognised her own body. She felt utter despair. She was constantly eating throughout the day and felt unable to stop. She confessed that she felt her life couldn't begin until she lost weight. Her self-sabotage didn't make sense—until you consider that she was seeing herself through her *mother's* eyes, all the while locked in the battle with her that she had been fighting since her teens. Melanie's overeating only hurt herself, but on some level, she was still doing it to spite her mother.

WHAT IS SHAME?

Shame is the feeling that, deep down, there is something wrong with us and that we are flawed. Shame can control our thoughts and actions to the extent that we, like Melanie, feel utterly powerless in our lives. Even if you're not aware of it, shame can affect your self-worth if you continue to carry it with you. But letting it go will release you from self-judgement and allow you to be the person you were born to be.

When you work on yourself, you don't completely change your default setting. You learn to understand it and work with it. Just like those uncomfortable feelings we learned to embrace in Chapter 9, shame must be cut down to size so that we are not controlled by it. You may never eliminate every trigger that makes you feel shame, but you can and must learn how to master those feelings and your responses to them. It is an ongoing process.

For most people, shame manifests as a deep, internal sense that something is wrong with them. Shame doesn't necessarily start with a parental interaction. It could develop from an encounter with a teacher or a general feeling of not fitting into a particular crowd. Shame makes you feel like an outsider who doesn't belong. All it takes to trigger it is an odd, unkind remark and a few giggles, and the seed is planted deep into our psyche, taking up permanent residence.

Shame can be very subtle beyond its initial sting. It often settles into a dull, low-level feeling that we usually aren't even aware of, but we still carry with us wherever we go. This general sense of uneasiness about not belonging affects our decisions, our activities, and our sense of self-worth.

We can probably all remember a moment in childhood where we felt shame at school. I have a very clear memory of being in the school choir when I was just ten years old. There were about fifty of us standing together practising a song, and suddenly the music teacher cut us off by saying, "Somebody is singing very out of tune, and it's ruining everything. It sounds like a cat screeching."

We sang the tune again and this time, she went around the room, putting her ear close to our mouths to hear which child was committing this crime. When she came to me, my heart was already hammering away from fear of the possible humiliation. The teacher stopped. I could feel all one hundred eyes in the room turn to stare at me.

"Katy, you are ruining this for everybody. Would you leave now?" she said, sharply.

I did the long walk of shame out of the hall, back to my class-room. I had learned that I was not good enough to sing, anytime or anywhere. For the next thirty years, I would literally mouth the song "Happy Birthday" at celebrations. Not until I had my babies did I find my voice again, and I enjoyed singing them lullabies.

In my own journey, moments of shame from childhood stayed

with me wherever I went, whatever I did, whatever I thought. As I began the deep work of reconnecting with my emotions, shame took the longest to reveal itself. I thought I didn't feel shame, yet it was at the very core of my being. It was the filter through which every thought passed, and I couldn't process it until I started to put the other tools discussed in the previous chapter into action. Eventually, as I peeled back layer after emotional layer, there was nowhere left for shame to hide.

SHAME AND GUILT

Shame is very different from guilt, though they often go hand in hand. Guilt is a feeling of responsibility or remorse for something you have done—or perceived you have done. Shame, on the other hand, is that feeling in the pit of your stomach where you just do not feel good enough: not slim enough, not bright enough, not wanted enough. While guilt comes from our actions and can be quite helpful in helping us correct those actions and behave differently next time, shame is the feeling that your whole self is irredeemably wrong.

Sometimes, guilt can lead to a positive outcome. For example, if we've said something we wish we hadn't or done something we wish didn't, we may feel guilty about it. This feeling prompts us to change our behaviour so we don't feel bad again. Guilt can lead to better choices, and is often released once you make amends and commit to doing better. Guilt is a result of our behaviour.

Shame, on the other hand, is not tied to our actions but to our sense of self. Unlike guilt, shame doesn't have any good outcome. Shame can control our feelings, our thoughts, and our actions.

It tells us we are not worthy of being loved and belonging. It makes us feel like an outsider looking in. It resigns us to remain spectators in our own lives: we watch everyone else having fun, all the while feeling like an imposter undeserving of that human connection.

Deep down, we overeat because of this persistent feeling that something is wrong with us. As we struggle to comfort ourselves or numb this deep sense of unworthiness, the act of eating itself causes shame. We know this is not what we should be doing.

We are then left in yet another vicious cycle: we eat to resolve our discomfort, which is often caused by the shame of overeating. The more we eat, the more shame we feel, and the cycle is never-ending.

Think about it: you are overeating to try to make yourself feel better when shame says you are not good enough, but then you are ashamed of the overeating. It defies logic—but shame isn't about logic or rational thought. It's an emotion that must be dealt with.

AWARENESS: GETTING TO THE ROOT OF OUR SHAME

I have mentioned that once shame has settled into our minds, it's often there to stay—unless you do something about it. It's the quiet houseguest that moves in and misplaces things like self-worth and self-love without letting us know. As we search and search for these things, we place ourselves on a destructive downward spiral.

We have to become aware of the thoughts that disrupt our

peace and pull us away from enjoying life. Once we recognise the repetitive nature of these thoughts, we can move towards healing. Take a look at the following questions to become more aware of how shame might be running the show in your own life:

- Are you the sort of person who says "sorry" to someone who has just stepped on *your* foot? In other words, do you reflexively apologise to someone who has hurt you?
- Are you someone who gets caught up in the terrible what-ifs before anything has actually happened?
- If you are short of money one month, do you catastrophise and automatically envision yourself out on the streets?
- If you feel unwell, do you immediately suppose you have a life-threatening illness?
- Are your antennae out? Are you hypervigilant and ready for disaster to strike?
- Do you look at people's facial expressions and imagine they are thinking the worst of you?
- Do you often feel like people say or think bad things about you?
- When you are invited to something, do you wonder if you were invited out of pity or obligation?

If you answered yes to some of the above questions, you are carrying around shame-based thoughts, and they are negatively impacting your life. We often think we can read people's minds, for example, but this "superpower" is imaginary. It amounts to convincing yourself that other people feel as critical about you as you do about yourself, and there is nothing magical or intuitive about it. This is how shame works. Remember, shame is the quiet houseguest that actively works behind the scenes—we are not even aware it's happening.

When we carry shame and don't think well of ourselves, we tend to expect the worst in life, as though we somehow deserve bad things happening to us. Whether we feel like a relationship is doomed, worry that we can't afford to send our toddlers to college, or think we are going to be homeless because of a budget miscalculation, we are projecting our shame into the future. When you always expect the worst, you have internalised a negative attitude and simply assume that's all you're going to get in life.

Here's a quick test. Have you ever said, "Why does everything bad always happen to me?" This is negative thinking as the default setting, and it can put you at risk of self-fulfilling prophecy if you continue to dwell on it. Shame is not easy to acknowledge, and it's even more difficult to admit that our own thoughts have been our worst enemy. But the awareness of your negative thinking is crucial to eventually take action to change it.

Let's look back to Melanie's story. Her shame was primarily rooted in her mother's constant criticism. Decades later, she still assumed she was a lousy parent and not good enough or deserving enough to lose weight, so she was much more likely to ruminate on those thoughts and allow other people to determine her value. The problem was that other people were *not* spending their days thinking about Melanie's self-worth. She was waiting for their validation, locked in a pattern of wanting to please that started with her mother. It's not easy to admit that you have allowed shame to run the show for most of your life, but once you do, shame starts to lose its power over you.

Your personal examples might be different. Perhaps you are fully confident at work, but you still feel the shame of overeating when you're home alone. Bearing shame doesn't mean that you constantly flit through life like a scared bunny rabbit—you may look like a lion on the surface, but still carry shame deep within. Becoming aware of what's beneath the surface is the key to moving forward.

ACCEPTANCE: YES, YOU FELL FOR IT

I want to unpack what it means to accept that shame has had a role in shaping your life and how you feel about yourself. This is where your ego may get in the way, because most of us probably don't think shame is part of our personality. We don't walk around wringing our hands and behaving like a doormat for everyone, so we must not feel shame, right? But that's not where shame resides.

Shame lives in the deep recesses of our minds and hearts, where it is so much a part of us that we struggle to locate it. In a strange way, you can also become quite self-centred when you carry shame, as it can manifest as the all-about-me syndrome. For example, if someone tells you they are not happy, you assume it has something to do with you and feel responsible for it—because you have those mind-reading skills, right? When you assign yourself blame for everything that is wrong, you are also placing yourself at the very centre of the universe, where every action and consequence revolves squarely around *you*.

It can be quite humbling to accept that this self-centred place is where your thoughts can take you. Instead, it's easier to blame others and rail against having drawn the short straw again—thoughts that can lead us directly to eating and the cycle of shame that the eating triggers.

The more you eat, the more shame you feel. And you fell for it.

None of us likes to admit that we have been bamboozled by shame. It has controlled us. It has slinked through our minds and our bodies, silently poisoning our thoughts, our perspectives, and our actions. You think people are as critical about you as you are, and since we judge our insides by other people's outsides, we always come out feeling second-best. Everything is pass-fail, black-and-white, and it can feel so much worse than it really is.

I used to see everything in extremes: no middle ground, no grey area that creates more choices. It's a zero-to-sixty line of thinking, a way of thinking that can lead you from having one date with someone who never called again to immediately thinking no one will ever ask you out again because you are so awful.

Shame always leads us to the big crescendo: *I'm not lovable, I'm always making stupid mistakes,* and so on. You're either on a diet and it's going brilliantly, or you are off the diet and everything is absolutely terrible. You still fell for it.

It can also make you feel overly responsible for other people and their feelings, which in turn makes you feel guilty when something doesn't work out. For example, your husband could come in from a long day's work and mention that he needs a bit of quiet. Immediately, shame arrives on the scene and you think, *What have I done? Why is he not being pleasant to me, or even talking to me?* It has nothing to do with you. Shame has us taking everything personally. You fell for that too.

But you are not stupid. You are not unlovable. You might have fallen for shame's insidious message, but many of us do. The difference is that you are intent on doing something about it—too many people never arrive at the moment of understanding and acceptance you have reached right now. Recognising that you fell for shame's lies and accepting that as a part of your life's journey is a humbling process.

On one hand, it's quite liberating to accept that someone else's problem isn't yours to solve, and that you are not at the centre of it. On the other hand, it is also humbling because you must admit—and accept—that until now you have been making their story all about you.

It may not seem that way at first. "I was trying to be a good friend," you may protest. Or, "If they loved me, they would want to tell me what happened, so I must have something to do with their mood." Unless you have blatantly insulted them or have breached their trust, it has nothing to do with you.

Instead, respect that they are in a temporary mood, accept that not everyone has to be your best friend, nor will you be everyone's best friend. We're not meant to carry the world on our shoulders while it revolves around us at the same time, but shame tells us otherwise.

That's why it feels like failure. But shame is a liar.

When you can identify where and when shame entered your universe and set you up to be the centre of it, you can figure out its hiding places. That may require you to accept that some bad or unfair things have happened to you, and this takes time. Once you see your shame for what it is, you must also accept responsibility for your own role in allowing that shame to control your life—how you've been self-centred and blaming others for your own thoughts. From there, you can start to re-evaluate the way you've been looking at the world.

ACTION: REPLACE SHAMEFUL THOUGHTS WITH LOVING AFFIRMATIONS

By now, I hope you are starting to push through and gently admit that maybe you are, in fact, doing some of what I have just described. You are taking notice and understanding: *This is me.*

What happens next? Better yet, what happens the next time that awful feeling of never being good enough bubbles to the surface?

You're going to practice what we learned in Chapter 2 and *take a pause.*

When you feel the first pangs of shame, try to understand what is happening before you get locked in the loop of negative thoughts and feelings. Are you having any negative physical or emotional effects? For example, where in your body do you feel this shame? Here are some examples of physical symptoms:

- Nausea
- Shaking
- Agitation
- Flushed face
- Goosebumps
- Hyperventilating
- Sweaty hands

- Clenched fists or jaw
- Dry mouth
- Headache

Whether you have some of these symptoms or others not listed here, it is helpful to recognise when shame is whispering a thought into your mind and momentarily press the pause button. The physical signs are often our first and clearest clue.

Next, ask yourself: Are these feelings justified? Should I feel guilty for something I have done wrong, or is this just shame telling me another lie?

Now, look at the evidence and information about what is really going on. Have you stepped into a judgement game, comparing yourself to other people? Are you assuming the worst out of habit? Could it be that someone actually invited you to a party because they like you? Or will all the so-called "evidence" you gather about those feelings wind up being merely your own thought patterns?

It takes time to move into a world of choices without extremes. We are so used to feeling uncomfortable and then looking for the solution in the food. By taking a pause, you have opened yourself up to new thoughts and perspectives. Using some of the coping strategies and tools you have learned in earlier chapters, ask yourself: *Where did I learn this negative self-talk?* Was it from other people's opinions, perhaps when you were younger? Better yet, do you hear someone else's voice—someone from your past—when the negative thoughts creep in? That may offer you a clue about where it originated.

Now, change that negative self-talk to a positive statement about yourself—and use your own name when you do it. Try these affirmations as a useful tool to begin to change your false beliefs:

- *[Your name] is lovable.*
- *[Your name] is precious.*
- *[Your name] is worthy of success.*
- *[Your name] has the right to be happy.*

When we slow down like this, we find peace. We begin to be the creators of our own lives. We can go after things we really want because we are worth it.

When we can accept shame as a part of us—but not the part that governs us—we can also see that we have value as human beings. We can feel good about ourselves, know we deserve the changes we are making, and reconnect with ourselves in an entirely new way.

BURST THE BUBBLE

Once we address the feelings churning beneath the eating, we make room for change. Then the next time you reach for food, the bubble of mindlessness has burst, and you have a chance to stop and make a different choice.

It is difficult to admit, much less accept, that you have been living under shame's control for so long, but now you can discover your *real* self. This is transformational. Finally, you are the person you were born to be, before you hid from the world and used food as a poor substitute for it. By embracing and feeling all that we are—which can be very painful at times—we can emerge as our own beautiful and imperfect selves.

For Melanie, this meant finally understanding how shame was steering the ship in her relationship with her mother. Once she accepted what was really driving her, she had the chance to reclaim her power. Melanie began to put some important boundaries in place to protect both herself and her relationship. For example, she limited the amount of time spent with her mother to reduce the opportunities for falling back into shame-based thinking and reacting. If there was a situation where she had to spend the whole day visiting, Melanie made sure she had a plan in place to allow for a bit of time out—typically walking the dog and having a friend give her a quick ring on her mobile.

In addition, Melanie put some support networks in place for herself. When her mother started in on her, Melanie would also remind herself that her mother was elderly and could not change. Any change that was to occur had to start and stop with Melanie herself, and that included her own perspective on their relationship.

Ultimately, Melanie had to accept her mother the way she was, if she was to have any sort of a relationship with her. It wasn't that her mother didn't love her. She just didn't know any other way to operate, because that's all she'd been shown by *her* mother. Melanie had arrived at a place where she understood and accepted that her mother was just doing the best she could with what she had.

This lightbulb moment helped Melanie find empathy, and she would use the mantra "this is not about me" whenever her mother criticised her. It made it much easier for her to simply ignore the comments that once would have sent her into a downward spiral of emotional eating. This made space for her to show her mother the sort of kindness she needed. But Melanie also understood that in extending that kindness, she was in no way responsible for fixing her mother's own problems.

As she began to see her mother as a human being rather than a fickle ruler who could never be pleased, Melanie could see this rather lonely lady who didn't have many friends, didn't have a great time in her own childhood, and was emotionally ill-equipped for happiness. Inside, part of Melanie was still that little girl who just wanted to feel the love of her mother. Once Melanie felt empowered to release her shame and open her eyes to new perspectives, she could let her guard down enough to notice her mother's smiles and the kind words buried among the critical comments.

It was such a relief for Melanie to stop giving her power away by trying to please other people. She finally understood that she didn't need to be locked in a battle that she would never win, harming herself along the way. Melanie stopped letting shame dictate the way she saw the world, and it changed her life.

As you get better about taking a time-out to see the truth of a situation—and stop the knee-jerk catastrophising and putting yourself at the centre of everything—it becomes much easier to do what is best for yourself. There is space for empathy instead of judgement, both for yourself and for others. As we begin to extend understanding to flawed people in our lives, we often find it much easier to treat our less-than-perfect selves with the same compassion. When you can hold a situation up to the light and see the reality of your life—not just your shame-skewed version of it—you will find the courage to love yourself just the way you are, and give yourself the good food that heals you.

Empowerment and self-love aren't selfish. They provide us the path to be the best versions of ourselves, which helps us be selective about our time, our relationships, and our choices. Taming the role of shame in our lives allows us to discover that we don't have to say *yes* to everything to please others.

CHAPTER 11

SAY NO TO SAY YES

When my sons were very young, it often felt like I had twelve children instead of just two. All day long, someone needed something. I was referee, nurse, chef, repair service, and more, all in the name of trying to give them a healthy, stable childhood.

It had been one of those days where I felt like I was wearing all of my hats all at the same time. One was hungry, one had broken a toy and cut his hand in the process, they both wanted me to read to them, and really, they just needed to get settled with a bit of food, a bath, and then into bed. That's when the phone rang.

"I need to talk," my mother choked out between sobs. "Can you come round this evening?"

I don't even have to tell you what the topic of conversation was. She was once again on the brink of leaving my stepfather, and she wanted me to rush over there to discuss it. The narrative never changed. I was always there for my mother when she was going through a relationship crisis, which happened at least a handful of times every year.

So now I was being asked to don another one of my hats: therapist. I had been wearing it since I was very young, so it felt like second nature. It was exhausting, but it was expected that I would still pack up my six-month-old baby and toddler son, put them in the car, and off we'd go to make sure she was okay.

I didn't even consider that I could say *no*. For many years, I just didn't feel like I had a choice. Despite desperately needing support as a mother, I did not pursue my own connections with other women my age to develop relationships with others in the same season in life. That's because I knew at any minute my mother might need me. Her expectation was that I would drop everything to rush over.

And I always did.

By the time this latest request came, however, I was already actively using some of the tools I've shared with you in this book: setting boundaries, taking the pause, and practising awareness, acceptance, and action. When she rang that day, it was the first time I realised how emotionally and mentally taxing this relationship was for me. I was on a rollercoaster with her, and it was taking its toll on me. I had two small, precious beings who were now my top priority—and that's as it should be. The last thing I needed was a trip that I already knew would put me on an even wilder mental ride. I just wanted to settle the children, give them their tea, and get them to bed.

"No," I heard my voice say.

PEOPLE-PLEASING VERSUS HELPING OTHERS

Remember, there is a reason the flight attendants instruct you to put your own oxygen mask on before you assist someone else with theirs. When you look after yourself, you actually look after those around you. In addition to keeping yourself strong for when they *truly* need you, taking care of your own needs also gives others the chance to build up support elsewhere. When they make more connections, they also benefit from a stronger network—and no single person is overburdened.

When I chose to look after myself that day, it changed the entire narrative. This dance with my mother wasn't doing either of us any good. It certainly was not changing or growing our relationship. It was not changing her relationship status, either—it's not like she was taking any of the advice she routinely asked me for. It was always the same: she'd relate her latest desperate tale of woe about something my stepfather had done, I'd rush over, we'd rehash it, she'd insist this time she was going to do something about it, and then she never would. It was all pointless.

I had been putting my own life on hold without even realising it. Any time I tried to take a stand with my mother (which, admittedly, wasn't very often), I would feel terrible because she was in such a terrible state. When I did see her, our visits always seemed to make her feel better. This, in turn, made me feel like I was responsible for lifting her spirits. She *needed* me. I was operating from a place of guilt rather than a healthy, mutually supportive place.

I'm really not sure why that particular day stood out as the day I would end the cycle. I was looking around my home at all that needed to be done: food to be cooked, toys to be tidied, children who needed to be fed, bathed, and put to bed. It all just felt over-whelming, and I could feel every fibre in my body screaming out to *not go.*

That *no* wasn't easy for me, and she was just as shocked as I was when I said it.

Shedding your physical weight sometimes requires you to shed your mental and emotional weight first. We need to learn how to get rid of the things that are holding us back so that we can embrace good things for ourselves. To do this, we need to make decisions that support what *we* need and want—not what others think we owe them.

Being a people-pleaser is a difficult thing to recover from. Now, there is certainly nothing wrong in doing things for other people. On the contrary, helping others can be wonderful and life-affirming. But giving from your heart, because you *want* to, is completely different from people-pleasing.

Years ago, my dear friend Anna rang me up in tears a month before I was due to get married. She was my bridesmaid.

"I just can't do it," she said. "I'm just too self-conscious. The idea that everyone would be looking at me? I feel so terrible, but I just can't go through with it."

"I think you might find they would actually be watching *me*, the bride," I joked. But Anna didn't laugh.

"I said *yes*, because it was such an honour to be asked, and I so wanted to be there for you," she said. "And I just felt it would be too rude to say *no*. Once I said *yes*, I didn't want to go back on my word, but I can't face doing it."

Fortunately, I had a group of dear old school friends. Another much-loved friend stepped in, even if she couldn't resist the should-have-asked-me-in-the-first-place smile.

It's easy to see, in this particular circumstance, that Anna would have taken better care of both herself and of me if she'd just said *no* in the first place, but hindsight is always a wonderful thing.

When I speak about people-pleasing, I mean putting other people's needs ahead of your own—to your own detriment. People-pleasing is the inability to say no, even though you know the burden you take on may be too much to bear. We run ourselves ragged to avoid making anyone else uncomfortable. But when we are run down and exhausted, it's a perfect storm for overeating. It's when we are overwhelmed and skipping vital self-care that we are most in danger of wanting a quick-fix and reaching for something outside ourselves for a temporary respite.

There are, of course, times in life where we must put others first, but that should be the exception and not the rule. People-pleasing normalises this sacrifice, and it is often rooted in insecurity.

We all want to fit in and belong. It makes us feel safer. We like the feeling of making other people happy. In the right amount, it makes us feel good about ourselves. But chronic people-pleasing is bloody exhausting. You are constantly saying *yes* to everything, just to please others—and to avoid dealing with the uncomfortable feelings that would surely come if you said *no*. In this regard, you're actually putting the opinions of others above your own and allowing your own self-worth to become contingent on making other people happy.

This is unsustainable. Fortunately, you can learn to say no by applying the skills of awareness, acceptance, and action when you are faced with a request to take on yet another responsibility. The key is to put some boundaries in place before you actually need them.

AWARENESS: WHEN YOU ARE UNABLE TO SAY NO

When setting a boundary, it is also important to be clear on your goals and what you want to achieve. If your goal is to lose weight, be selective about saying *yes* in ways that support you in this goal. If something holds you back or distracts you from this goal, be aware that you are blazing a new trail, and the familiar path will not help you reach your destination. Make choices that support *your* goals—it's not selfish, rude, or unkind to others.

We may want to remain in good standing with others, but our sacrifice also deflects us from addressing our own feelings. Boundaries, on the other hand, teach other people how to treat us with respect. When we have boundaries in place, we can better honour the commitments that we *have* made. This is very important, because boundaries make us more selective about how our time is used, and for whom. There is value in our choices, but it's up to us to set that value.

Answer the following statements by agreeing or disagreeing:

· I find it difficult to say *no* to people.

- I feel guilty or uncomfortable when I say *no* to good friends because I want to be liked.
- I don't want to say *no* in case it stirs up conflict.
- When making plans with friends, I often go along with their suggestions.
- I don't like to say *no* in case it gives somebody else difficulty.
- I don't like to say *no* because I don't want to disappoint somebody.
- I feel rude if I say *no* after I already said *yes*.
- Sometimes when I say *yes* I regret it, and then I feel resentful.

If you agreed with any of these, then you are likely not helping others. You are people-pleasing.

It's a good idea to get clarity on these issues as we learn to say *no*. Like a new pair of shoes, setting a boundary may feel uncomfortable at first, because it puts us out of our comfort zone. But why do we settle for a "comfort zone" that fills us with dread, regret, or resentment? What's comforting about that? We are settling for what is familiar—not what's healthy for ourselves.

The next time you are asked to do something, do not reply immediately. Buy yourself some time to reflect and become aware of your true feelings about the request and what it will require of you.

Here are some phrases to help you avoid the pitfalls of people-pleasing:

- "Let me get back to you."
- "I need time to think about that."
- "I have to check my calendar."

This gives you time to determine the *real* cost of saying *yes*. Draft a pros and cons list if that helps. By putting a pause between the request and your response, you have time to evaluate your time and your energy and see the consequences more clearly.

It is important to honour the commitments that you accept, but it is also your right to refuse them as a means to protect yourself from over-commitment. If you say *yes* when you really want to say *no*, you are really saying that someone else's opinion of you is more important than your opinion about yourself. So in essence, you are saying that they are more important than you.

When you become more aware of your people-pleasing tendencies, you can change this dynamic and begin to put your own needs first.

ACCEPTANCE: BE YOUR OWN BEST FRIEND FIRST

This is where the rubber meets the road. You've said no, and someone acts annoyed, perhaps rolling their eyes or heaving a world-weary sigh in your direction. You have to accept that this person is used to you saying yes and may not appreciate your change in attitude. You cannot control other people's reactions and feelings about your choices. Keep going. Follow your heart and pay attention to your gut feelings about what is right and what is healthy for you.

This takes practice, especially if people are used to you being their go-to person. Teaching people how to respect you and how to treat you properly is hard work.

When someone responds with annoyance, or even anger, it's

not going to feel great. You'll second-guess whether you made the right decision, wondering whether you were short-sighted, if that person will remain annoyed with you forever, and if this somehow makes you a selfish person.

Trust that you did make the right decision. They may get over it—and if they don't, it's not your job to make everything alright. I know it doesn't feel good right now, but you are climbing out of a people-pleasing pit of regret and resentment for all those times you said *yes* in the past. The closer you get to the light, the better you will feel.

To strengthen your resolve, try the following exercise. Close your eyes and think about someone who is always making requests of your time and energy. Maybe they are a strong personality who persuades you into it; maybe they are a needy personality who guilts you into it. Regardless, imagine looking that person straight in the eye and simply saying *no*. Do not attempt to justify or explain your decision. Just envision yourself looking directly at them, telling them *no*, and letting that be that.

What is happening in your body right now? Do a quick scan. Do you feel tension? Do you feel sick? Is your heart pounding or your stomach turning?

You can calm your physical response by practising some 4-7-8 breathing: breathing in for four seconds, holding for seven seconds, and exhaling for eight seconds. This breathing exercise is also a great tool to use prior to a difficult conversation to get relaxed and focused. If you feel yourself slipping into *yes* mode whilst in conversation, you can excuse yourself for a moment, find a private spot, and do your 4-7-8 breathing then and there.

Doing so will provide the pause you need to allow the uncomfortable physical feelings to rise and pass through you.

The physical feelings may be uncomfortable, but they provide valuable information. They let you know that you are claiming your power. You are no longer going to be the yes-person, the one who gives, the one who is taken from. You are taking on the new role of being your own best friend—and there will be those who don't like it. They want you to remain as you were, as that works for them.

Sometimes, we must accept that those who claim to love us are also, either directly or indirectly, sabotaging our progress.

Erica was a client who had been making excellent progress on her weight loss when she hit a plateau. Although Erica was a grown woman with children of her own, she still worried about her mother's opinion of her. Erica's mother didn't like the physical change in her daughter and kept bringing sugary treats over to her house. She would then act hurt if Erica said *no* or only took a small bite.

Now, this isn't unusual. As soon as the weight begins to drop off, the people around you won't always support the change. Most of the time, they are not deliberately trying to sabotage your weight loss, but somehow the transformation in you makes them uncomfortable. For whatever reason, Erica's mother wanted things to go back to the way they were before the weight loss— hence the unending bags of sweets, cakes, and biscuits making an appearance.

When Erica finally said to her mother, "No thanks. I don't want these in the house," it was a big deal. She had rehearsed for this moment many times. Having her mother's approval was important to her, but Erica's simple *no* brought an emotional release that led to the release of her weight, too. Although her mother didn't like it, Erica's *no* led to lasting change. It wasn't easy, but it set her free. The plateau she had been stuck on disappeared, and the weight started coming off again.

Some people feel hurt when you politely decline their offer of food or treats. When someone says to you, "One won't hurt," they are testing your boundaries. All you have to do is smile and say no thanks. If they continue to push it, breathe and say, "Thank you, but I'm okay without it." It will be awkward, but remain pleasant, even if your heart is pounding inside your chest. People want you to stay the same, because change is scary. It will be up to you to teach them to respect your boundaries.

It is natural to want to avoid making waves that will make you feel uncomfortable—that's how you end up saying *yes* and then wishing you hadn't. Remember, feelings are temporary. It can also be difficult to accept that we are not responsible for another person's feelings or behaviours, only our own.

Most of our loved ones would insist they are not trying to sabotage anything we do to improve ourselves, but there is an underlying fear that whatever we are doing will disrupt the relationship dynamic—whether healthy or dysfunctional. It could also bring up an uncomfortable awareness of their own habits that they'd rather not face. Learn to be your own best friend, best parent, or best sibling to protect the relationship you have with yourself. Saying *yes* to you often requires saying *no* to others—and that's okay.

ACTION: TELL THE TRUTH FIRMLY AND POLITELY

I will say it again: You have the right to say no.

Now it's time to build and flex those muscles. You have been too busy being over-committed, overworked, and overwhelmed. Establishing the boundary of *no* is one thing; actually saying it in a way that is kind and courteous takes a bit of finesse.

For starters, there is no need to make things up to smooth things over or manipulate the situation. If this chapter has opened your eyes to ways you have been manipulated into saying yes in the past, why would you want to use the same strategy on someone else? That's not healthy at all. Lying can also backfire, as we tie ourselves in knots because we might not remember what we said and end up telling more lies in the future. Lying is totally unnecessary.

Then there is the so-called art of being vague. That doesn't help the other person, either. It usually raises the stakes for them to put pressure on you to meet their needs, especially if you have a history of saying *yes* to them. Phrases like, "we'll see" and "that's something to think about" only kick the can down the road. The other person will eventually come back to you with higher expectations and stronger demands because you were vague enough to make them think you were entertaining the idea.

When you say *no*, you must be firm about it. Here are some useful phrases to have on standby as you stand up for your own needs:

- "I don't have time."
- "I have a lot going on at the moment."

- "Sorry, I can't."
- "Unfortunately, it's not a good time."

Remember, you don't have to go into loads of detail or make excuses when you say *no*. That gives the impression that you somehow owe an explanation, which you don't. Be confident in your decision. There's no need to justify your choice. Once your no is definitive, you do not owe anyone a lengthy, detailed explanation. There is nothing vague about a definitive *no*, and it's up to you whether you want to provide any additional details.

Think of it this way: You are saying *no* to them and *yes* to yourself. Saying *no* is a form of self-care.

My client Sue has a story that is all too familiar for many young mothers. As the mother of two young children, she worked part-time, always felt tired, and just didn't feel like she had the time to prepare good meals for herself.

As a result, Sue constantly ate the children's leftovers, like the crusts of their toasts in the morning. She would graze while on the move or tidying up, but her nutrition always came last on her to-do list throughout the day. While she didn't articulate it, it was obvious to me that she didn't feel she deserved to sit down and have a proper meal.

Each week, Sue volunteered at her children's school to help pupils learn to read, and she enjoyed it. Now the school was ringing her more and more, asking her to take on more responsibility, organise events, and help out with field trips.

Sue was at breaking point. Each time the school called, they told her how desperate they were for volunteers. They needed her so! And there it is, the thing that sucks us in: *the need to be needed.*

Of course there are times in life when we do things we don't want to because it's for the greater good, but this was becoming a pattern with a negative effect on Sue's peace of mind and health. She was always exhausted and overwhelmed. When we role-played saying *no* to the school, Sue initially gave me a five-minute answer, listing all the reasons she couldn't do it. Her voice climbed as she spoke, reaching a desperate, "please understand me" pitch.

We worked and worked to keep her response short, direct, and kind. No apologies.

The next time they called, Sue felt such a huge relief when she said, "No, I'm not available at that time." From then on, she also made a point to do something just for herself every day. As a result, Sue felt more in control of her life and was happier because she made more time for herself.

And the weight came off.

SAYING NO TO FOOD

When you're offered treats and decline, don't be surprised if you are met with resistance. In our culture, there's a lot of meaning in the giving and receiving of food, and we often feel social pressure to take whatever we are offered to avoid hurting someone's feelings. This comes from a good place, but when you're not the kind of person who can stop with just one bite, you need to create a clear boundary.

Some hosts may push you to eat by saying how delicious it is or even telling you about all the effort that went into making it, ordering it, or something like that. When this happens, just smile and say:

- "Thanks, I'm going to pass."
- "Thank you, but I'm not hungry right now."
- "Thank you, but I'm okay without it."
- "It looks fabulous, and smells wonderful. But I will pass this time."
- "Wow, I'll bet that did take a lot of time to make, but I just don't have room for it right now."

Your heart may be hammering and you may feel awkward, but you can do it. Teach people to respect your boundaries, and it will get easier every time.

TIME TO MOVE FORWARD

When you learn how to say *no*, you are saying *yes* to yourself. And when you are more selective about saying *yes* to others, your *yes* holds more value.

We only have so much time and energy, so we have to be mindful and make our decisions accordingly. When we look after ourselves first, it produces a ripple effect, and we actually have more energy to give to others—energy that comes from the heart. If we allow ourselves to become rundown and fail to pause and reflect on what we really want, it becomes much more difficult to make good choices about food.

Try saying *yes* to yourself first. Any additional *yes* you give to others should be honest, feel wonderful, and come from a place of joy.

Once upon a time, I felt responsible for my mother's happiness. I never wanted to upset her by saying *no*. Of course, that made her rely on me even more, instead of learning how to strengthen her own resolve to follow through on her decisions. By freeing up the time I once spent soothing her, I was able to develop better relationships with other mothers and build new friendships for myself and my children. It also meant that my mother and I had more time to do joyful things together rather than focus on aspects of her life that I could not fix.

If you have a history of people-pleasing, set the expectation for yourself that setting boundaries and saying no will be a bit uncomfortable at first. If the other person tries to argue your decision, remember that you don't have to make excuses. You don't have to keep justifying your decision to them. A simple "No, it's not a good time for me at the moment," should suffice. Stick to your guns. You are worth it.

CHAPTER 12

NOW, IT'S ABOUT FOOD

One day when I was in my twenties, working in London, I went to a café to eat lunch. I was dieting again, so I ordered an uninteresting salad and started people-watching.

A couple of young women close to my age sat at the next table, and they were sharing a slice of chocolate cake. As I watched them chat and occasionally dip their respective forks into the cake, a bell went off in my head: I noticed that they weren't concerned about the cake as much as they were about each other.

Now even I, the overeater at the time, had occasionally shared a pudding with someone. The difference was that, whenever I split a dish with someone, I was in a race that my counterpart wasn't even aware they were taking part in. I was just trying to get as much food as possible without being obvious about it.

There was definitely no eating competition going on here, because neither of these young women seemed very intent on the cake. They just had a bite here and there, then would put their forks down and have a bit of a laugh. One might pick up her fork, take another odd bite, then continue the conversation. In the end, they both put down their forks, leaving half of the cake still on the plate as they carried on talking.

I was completely engrossed at that point. *Did they not realise half of the cake is still there? What is going on here?* The cake was not their main event. It had no power over either of them, and it only enhanced what was already there: the conversation and the friendship. What was crystal clear to me at that moment was *I'm not one of them, because I would not leave a crumb on that plate.* I was always ready to eat more.

THE RACE IS ON

You may well know the race I just described. You try to appear casual so as not to arouse suspicion from your unwitting competitor, but you are absolutely intent on getting as much of that shared dessert, plate of fries, or appetiser as possible. You just don't relate to food the way other people do.

We have spent most of this book detailing how weight loss requires more focus on *you*—getting to know yourself and using the tools to stop overeating—and less focus on food as the root of your problems. But now we have to focus on the food itself. Having walked through the mental and emotional impact of overeating, we have painfully stripped away layers of shame to figure out where our relationship with food derailed. Now that you see your eating for what it really is, it's time to rebuild a new, healthy relationship with food.

To do this, we are going to examine the physiological effect of certain types of food to understand why so much of what you eat is actually *designed* to enable your overeating. I will provide information designed to help you build your own boundaries about what you choose to put in your body. This is not about suggesting that yours is a future filled with iceberg lettuce (unless you happen to like iceberg lettuce). This is about savouring food and making choices that work with your body, not against it. This is about empowering you to make informed choices about food that will nourish your body and give it what it *really* needs— which ultimately assists your mental and emotional health too.

SUGAR'S NOT-SO SWEET SIDE

When I was a child, my brother and I would take our pocket money and go to the local sweet shop. I would eat my bag of sweets in one sitting and then spend the rest of the day hankering after his.

My brother's package always contained dark chocolate—a treat practically unheard of for a child in the 1970s. He slowly savoured the more complex, slightly bitter treat. He'd sample just a little bit, and then put the rest away for later. I mean, who does that?

Other people, not me. At least not back then. These types of treats used to call to me, even if they were in another room, but I don't have that challenge anymore. Now I can have all sorts of food in the house and not get triggered. But for decades of my life, this was a problem, so I understand the call of certain foods all too well.

First, I want you to know that the power these foods have over you is not all in your head. Processed and sugary foods can be addictive, in the sense that the more you consume, the more you want, because you are never satisfied. Understanding the complexities of how sugar works in the brain and the body will help you make more informed choices moving forward.

For our ancient ancestors, sugar was a rare treat, so when they came across some honey or a briar packed with berries, it was in their best interest to eat as much as possible. Our genes were programmed to love those rare sugars and seek them out to help us survive. But today we are bombarded by sweet treats at every turn. When we eat sugar, such as a chocolate bar, our body pumps out the hormone called insulin, which levels our blood-sugar back to normal. Our bodies are designed to cope with a sweet treat like this every now and then, just as the occasional berry jackpot would have been fine for a hunter-gatherer.

When we eat too much sugar, however, our bodies can become insulin-resistant. Then we need more and more of it to have the same effect. We can become insulin-resistant without even knowing it. A consequence of insulin resistance is that fat cells can't release their stored energy into the bloodstream, where the fatty acids could be used as fuel. So insulin resistance means more fat on your body. Sugar, then, is something we want to avoid, or at least consume in much smaller quantities. Some sugar is obvious in our diets: sweets, puddings, and the like are clearly packed with the stuff. But there are also plenty of hidden sugars that are trickier to avoid.

Now, we need to pause here because I want to acknowledge that you are human. You like pleasure. I totally get it. When your blood sugar gets low, you want something that will give you a quick hit of energy, and you will crave the very thing that has caused the problem in the first place: sugar. The rush of sugar from a chocolate bar alerts the reward centres in your brain to release feel-good neurotransmitters such as dopamine. These endorphins surge to give you intense pleasure. What's not to like? It provides an instant hit of energy...until you crash. Then, you feel tired, irritable, guilty, and full of sugar cravings again.

This is not your fault. It is a physical reaction. You've been on a never-ending rollercoaster, and sugar has been the primary operator, working all the controls. Are you ready to get off the ride?

AWARENESS: THE PROFITS AND LOSSES OF SUGAR CONSUMPTION

Without awareness of our physical and emotional needs, we are almost powerless to resist sugar's seduction. In fact, the food manufacturers are counting on it. Food manufacturers hijack our cravings, and processed foods have your cravings baked right in. This added sugar is often concealed under different names, masquerading in unexpected places.

One way sugar disguises itself is in flour. Did you know that processed wheat quickly turns to sugar in the body? White flour is made almost entirely from the endosperm, the starchy centre of the wheat, that has very little of the actual kernel left. This enables it to convert quickly to glucose and take you on that sugary rollercoaster ride.

When it's not disguised as flour, sugar often uses an alias to throw unsuspecting shoppers off the scent. Check the labels of your favourite snacks for these other names for sugar:

- Sugar cane
- Caramel
- Corn syrup
- Dextrin
- Dextrose
- Fructose
- High-fructose corn syrup
- Dextrin
- Maple syrup
- Molasses
- Ethyl maltol
- Rice syrup
- Orbital sucrose
- Maltodextrin
- Barley malt
- Maltose
- Sorbitol

Believe me, this is just a starter list, and it can be hard to keep up without a chemistry degree. But even if you don't read your ingredient labels in full, it's fair to say that if you are eating processed or prepackaged food, there is a very high chance that sugar is in there—even in so-called "diet" foods.

And then, there are all these artificial sweeteners that we think are healthier. We think we've beaten the system by getting the sweet hit without the calories, but your body doesn't know the difference and reacts the same way. Artificial sweeteners do not get you off the rollercoaster, because your brain still craves hit after hit of sweetness, keeping you constantly wanting more.

It doesn't matter if you have eaten something obviously sugary like cake, some hidden sugars in processed food, or an artificial sweetener—when we overeat these foods, it sets us off on a blood-sugar rollercoaster. And we lose.

A good rule of thumb? If it is mass-produced in a factory, it's best to avoid it. I don't care how grandmotherly the woman on the label appears, or how athletic the smiling couple on the nutrition bar seems. That's all just marketing—as are labels like "healthy," "diet," and even "sugar-free." Take the time to read the list of ingredients, and the moment you stumble upon a word you can't pronounce or understand—especially if the word ends in -ose—consider putting it back on the shelf. It's a ticket to the rollercoaster, and once your taste buds are hijacked, you'll just crave more.

Now that you are fully aware of all the places sugar might be lurking, it's time to carry that awareness with you throughout daily life. So each time you reach for a packaged food in response to a craving, press the pause button and scan the label. Each time you take a moment to search for hidden sugar, you are presenting yourself with an opportunity to make a better choice. That choice is to get off the rollercoaster instead of thinking, "Tomorrow, I'll stop. Tomorrow, I'll be good."

You are empowered to do it *now*, not tomorrow—you just weren't aware that you held the keys.

ACCEPTANCE: YOU ARE UNIQUE, FOR BETTER OR WORSE

Now that you are fully aware of sugar's effects, part of your healing is to accept the way your body handles it. Remember that if you have difficulty stopping once you've started eating processed foods, it's not a moral failing. Your brain and your body are wired this way.

The physical and mental effects of sugar vary greatly from person to person, so it's important to understand how sugar affects *you*.

QUIZ: HOW DOES SUGAR AFFECT YOU?

Answer the following questions with a simple *yes* or *no*:

- Do you feel intense cravings for sugary treats?
- Do you feel bloated when you eat sugary treats?
- Do you have stubborn belly fat that seems immune to your weight loss efforts?
- Are you often irritable or moody?
- Do you have generally low energy?
- Do you have trouble focusing?
- Do you feel sluggish a couple of hours after eating?

If you answered yes to most of these questions, you have a problem with sugar. It's time to accept that your relationship with sugar may not be like everyone else's—but you can make choices that work with *your* body to get the results you want.

When you eat sugar—whether obvious or hidden—you experience a physiological reaction. This will never change. While some people can eat some sugar and not experience negative effects, others cannot bounce back from the rollercoaster ride. I know, because this is me.

The only solution is to accept that this is simply how your body works and resolve to wean yourself away from unhealthy food. This may seem daunting, but the best way to handle it is to clear the pantry and fridge of all sugary products. It's easy to be tempted if it's there, so don't allow opportunities for snacking on processed food and sugary treats.

This is a big step, but the important thing to remember is that this is not about being deprived. It is about the power of making informed choices that align with your goals. It's about stepping away from the choices that lead to misery and moving towards the choices that make you feel lighter, both on and off the scale.

If you want to support your weight loss goals, accept the fact that your go-to comfort foods do not work with your body. When you can accept that you will have to handle things a bit differently than the friend who can be happy with just an occasional slice of cake, you can begin to take action. As you move forward with actions that will actually help and not hinder your goals, you will usher peace into your life.

ACTION: A NEW APPROACH TO FOOD

Now that you are aware of just how much sugar is hidden in your diet and have accepted how these processed foods affect your wellbeing, it's time to take action. See what's in your pantry and take inventory of how much your food is processed or packaged. What steps will you take to eliminate them from your daily food intake?

It's not enough to simply throw out all of your sweet treats and processed foods—though this is, for many of us, a necessary starting point. But what will you eat when those foods are gone?

Taking effective action means making better choices, for both *what* you eat and *how* you eat it.

WHAT TO EAT

Making healthy food choices should not be all about deprivation. That's a recipe for failure. Instead of thinking about what you *can't* eat, embrace what you *can* eat. One easy way to manage that mental shift is to think in terms of "eating the rainbow." When we eat the rainbow, we are consuming all colours of healthy fruits and vegetables: red apples, leafy greens, yellow peppers, and so on. See the chart below to get inspired by the variety available to you:

The Rainbow of Healthy Foods

RED	ORANGE	YELLOW	GREEN	PURPLE	WHITE
radishes	pumpkin	peppers	avocado	cabbage	shallots
raspberries	squash	ginger	broccoli	cauliflower	onions
red onions	peaches	lemons	asparagus	prunes	cauliflower
red pepper	apricots	bananas	artichoke	plums	turnips
watermelon	cantaloupes	corn	celery	olives	fennel
tomato	carrots	grapefruit	cabbage	grapes	parsnips
strawberries	mangoes	starfruit	courgette	figs	garlic
rhubarb	nectarines	pineapple	cucumber	blueberries	leeks
pomegranate	oranges	pears	green beans	aubergine	mushrooms
cranberries	peppers		cabbage	blackberries	coconut
apples	papaya		salad greens	beetroot	
	sweet potatoes		peppers	cherries	
			kiwi		
			kale		
			limes		
			okra		
			peas		
			Brussels sprouts		

The good news is that you don't have to memorise the chart above or get bogged down with nutritional details. This is not a diet, but a mindset change. Just keep it simple:

· **Eat the rainbow** both cooked and raw, with fresh fruits and salads.
· **Embrace natural, high-quality fats** like olive oil, butter, and coconut oil.
· **Eat plenty of protein** in each meal.

This strategy will provide long-term energy instead of the short bursts and crashes that you get with sugar. Protein actually reduces your appetite because it reduces your level of the hunger hormone ghrelin. It also boosts the levels of peptide YY, a hormone that makes you feel full and can actually decrease your cravings too.[8] As a bonus, protein only minimally impacts your blood sugar, so you don't have to worry about riding the rollercoaster of energy spikes and crashes throughout the day.

Likewise, healthy fats reduce your appetite by slowing the release of sugar into your bloodstream to help stabilise your blood sugar level. They also trigger satiety signals to tell your brain you are full. Our bodies thrive on these good fats, and they have been part of our diet for millions of years. Your body is designed to thrive on them—in moderation, of course.

Finally, loading up on fruits and vegetables ensures that you get all the nutrition you need. Different coloured foods contain different phytonutrients, all of which have different benefits for your body.[9] No one colour is superior to another, which is why a balance of all colours is important. The fibre in these fruits and vegetables helps regulate your blood sugar and feeds the healthy bacteria in your gut, which supports a strong immune

8   Marion Journel et al., "Brain Responses to High-Protein Diets," *Advances in Nutrition* 3, no. 3 (January 2012): 322–329, https://doi.org/10.3945/an.112.002071.

9   Katherine D. McManus, "Phytonutrients: Paint Your Plate with the Colors of the Rainbow," *Harvard Health Blog,* Harvard Health Publishing, Harvard Medical School, April 25, 2019, https://www.health.harvard.edu/blog/phytonutrients-paint-your-plate-with-the-colors-of-the-rainbow-2019042516501.

system.[10] We thrive when we eat the variety of natural foods that both satisfy and nourish us.

Cutting back on sugar and embracing healthier foods will be challenging for several days to two weeks—your body has to detox, after all—so give yourself some time. The hunger pangs and cravings will pass. During this time, be kind to yourself with self-care strategies from Chapter 7 to distract you for a bit while your body adjusts. You'll also want to support your body by drinking plenty of water during this transition.

When we begin to cut down on our processed, packaged food consumption, we can make a concerted effort to increase real food, whole food, the kind that grows or is raised naturally. People who eat fewer processed foods reportedly experience improved concentration, higher quality sleep, and better moods within weeks.[11]

And here's a bit more good news: You can eat more when you eat this way! Pile your plate with different vegetables and leafy greens, have butter and olive oil, and enjoy a protein that is about the size and thickness of the palm of your hand. I'm not encouraging you to overeat, but that is a lot more food for a lot less cost to your body!

---

10 Annett Klinder et al., "Impact of Increasing Fruit and Vegetables and Flavonoid Intake on the Human Gut Microbiota," *Food & Function* 7, no. 4 (2016): 1788–1796. https://doi.org/10.1039/c5fo01096a.

11 Joseph Firth et al., "Food and Mood: How Do Diet and Nutrition Affect Mental Wellbeing?," *Food for Thought 2020, BMJ* 369 (2020): m2382. https://doi.org/10.1136/bmj.m2382.

FOOD: A STARTER GUIDE

What we eat affects our health, our mood, and our body. Some people are capable of cutting back on triggering foods; for others, eliminating something entirely is better. If you are looking for help drawing boundaries for your eating, consider these actions.

Reduce or eliminate:

- Bread
- Muffins
- Biscuits
- Bagels
- Cereal
- Baked goods
- Pancakes
- White sugar
- Chocolate bars
- Crackers
- Crisps
- Milkshakes
- Anything else made with flour or sugar

Embrace:

- Protein: fish, chicken, turkey, pork, lamb, beef, shellfish, beans, eggs, and cheese
- Fruits and vegetables: see the *Rainbow of Healthy Foods* chart
- Natural fats: animal fats, avocados, butter, coconut oil, olives, and olive oil
- Nuts
- Seeds
- Fresh herbs

HOW TO EAT

There's more to healthy eating than the foods you choose. You also need to become more *mindful* while you eat. As we discussed in Chapter 5, mindfulness leads to a whole host of benefits for your mind and body. *Mindful eating* has the power to transform your relationship with food for good.

For one thing, when we become more aware of the textures, flavours, and colours of our meals, we are more likely to savour the food when we sit down to eat. That doesn't happen when we throw a box in the microwave or tear open a bag of crisps and shift our minds to something else. As you take the time to really think about what you put in your body and expand your eating to include natural, colourful, healthful foods, you will also begin to rewire your brain and body to work together more harmoniously at mealtime.

One key to this mind-body shift is leptin. Our bodies need to know that we are eating in order to release this hormone, which lets your brain know when you are full. We don't want to ignore these signs, so try these practical tips to optimise your meal times and signal to your body that you are eating:

- Make a habit to always sit down and eat off a plate—never from fridge or pantry to mouth!
- Don't eat while working at the computer. Instead, focus squarely on enjoying the meal.
- Likewise, don't eat whilst scrolling through your phone. It's much harder to pay attention to how much and how quickly you eat when you are distracted.
- Eat slowly to develop the awareness to know when you are

full. When you eat too quickly, you're not giving your hormonal system time to signal that you are full.
- Chew thoroughly. This will stop you bolting your food down and help you listen to your body.
- Really notice and savour the aroma, texture, and flavour of the food.
- Remember to drink water throughout the day. Sometimes thirst can be mistaken for hunger.

These habits will make mindless eating a thing of the past. When you eat, stay present. It will make a difference.

Another main component of mindfulness is being vigilant about how much food you take in each day. Portion control is a major key to healthy weight loss, and you must remain aware of how much you consume to take control of your life.

When it comes to portions, you must set boundaries for yourself. Boundaries provide clarity and can be really helpful if your problem is always wanting more and never knowing when you've had the last mouthful. I recommend the following portion sizes when you're building your lunch or dinner plate:

	FOR WOMEN	FOR MEN
PROTEIN	5 oz. cooked chicken, meat, or fish	6 oz. cooked chicken, meat, of fish
	OR	OR
	2 eggs	3 eggs
	OR	OR
	2 oz. cheese	3 oz. cheese
VEGETABLES	5 oz. cooked vegetables	6 oz. cooked vegetables
	AND	AND
	5 oz. salad	6 oz. salad
FRUIT	1 piece	1 piece
FATS	1.5 Tbsp. oil, butter, mayonnaise, or ranch dressing	1.5 Tbsp. oil, butter, mayonnaise, or ranch dressing
OPTIONAL STARCH OR GRAIN	2 oz. potato or rice	2 oz. potato or rice

While the portions above make sense for lunch and dinner, many of my clients have struggled with what to eat for breakfast. You can keep it simple with a bowl of oatmeal topped with Greek yoghurt and fruit and a boiled egg on the side. If you'd like to get more creative, try a roast vegetable frittata with citrus on the side. The main thing is to move away from sugary cereals, muffins, and toast.

HOW TO GET STARTED

When we reach for food, it's often the quickest and easiest things that we grab—and that usually means consuming low-quality items. But when you are no longer basing your food choices on your emotions, it frees you up to make healthier choices that are aligned with your goals.

Making good choices on a consistent basis takes preparation: you must have a plan to succeed. Good intentions mean nothing without action, and all the courageous emotional work that you are doing will not lead to the outcomes you desire if you don't also have the right food on hand to support you.

The good news is that this is not about living on lettuce. You are moving away from calorie counting and unsustainable dieting and moving towards choices that work with your body. When you follow the recommendations above, you get to plan extremely varied and satisfying meals—but the key is that you do have to *plan.*

To begin, start by planning your meals in advance—breakfast, lunch, and dinner. If you wait until the moment you're hungry to decide what you want to eat, you'll be pushed towards unhealthy choices. Instead, plan your meals around the portions and healthy foods listed above. Leave nothing to chance! I recommend getting a little notebook to write down your shopping list and what you will eat each day.

Once you've planned your meals, make your shopping list. You can start by checking for what's already available in your pantry and refrigerator, then filling in what you need for your cooking. You should also consider having quick options from the list above on hand in case you find yourself heading out for a long day of errands or an unexpected trip. This will help you avoid the temptation of junk food when you're out and about.

Exhaustion makes it difficult to make decisions—it's why retailers place chocolate and snacks close to the cash registers to take advantage of shoppers' decision fatigue at the end of their trip.

Choosing what you're going to eat the night before or first thing in the morning can combat decision fatigue, because you have the time to plan your meals while you're fresh. This saves you from sudden food choices based on emotion, exhaustion, or overwhelm.

If the food choices available at work are not good, take your own. When it comes to packing your lunches, the easiest thing is to make an extra portion of your dinner the night before to bring with you. Otherwise, just think about what you would usually put on a dinner plate: a portion of protein, lots of veggies, and a serving of healthy fat.

You can make packing a lunch go quickly by stocking up on tins of tuna or batch cooking and slicing some chicken breasts, salmon, or boiled eggs in advance. Roasting vegetables like pumpkin, carrots, and sweet potatoes with some peppers and leeks will also save you time. Once you have all the ingredients at hand, throwing together a packed lunch becomes quite easy.

More good news: you can also still go out to eat *and* make good choices at the same time. When you're meeting friends for lunch or dinner, hop online and review the menu. There's bound to be a delicious option in line with the food that works for your body, so choose it! Plan in advance how you will order, and you won't even have to ask any questions when you arrive.

I understand this can all sound daunting at first, but when you've done it a few times, meal planning and portable lunches will just become part of your routine. The pull towards food can feel like a magnet, but these action steps are going to break this pattern by creating new habits and boundaries.

This is about putting yourself first, even if it takes some extra time to begin with. It's amazing how many mothers I worked with who would easily find time for their children if they needed a packed lunch or even a last minute fancy dress costume—they wouldn't think twice about just getting it done. Yet these same women had to remind themselves that they were worthy of the bit of extra time to get a delicious lunch together for themselves.

You can do this. You are worth the care and attention. Preparing beautiful meals is a form of self-care that you absolutely deserve.

WHAT DOES YOUR BODY NEED?

Enjoying a delicious, nourishing meal—one full of proteins and plenty of colourful vegetables—really helps stop the fridge shuffle. By eating three balanced meals and an occasional healthy snack, we never become ravenous, nor are we uncomfortably full. This strategy staves off hunger pangs, so the constant, mindless nibbling and grazing are less likely to occur. Your body is maintaining homeostasis.

It's not about dieting. It's about giving your body what it needs. If you eat a lot of processed food, you can actually become malnourished, which ironically leads to overeating as the body desperately tries to take in whatever nutrients it can find. In this case, it doesn't matter how many crisps you've had—you'll still be hungry twenty minutes later because you haven't actually given your body what it needs. Remember, proper nutrition is a form of self-care.

When I think about that moment in the café so many years ago, knowing that I could never leave a bite of cake on a plate, the common denominator between me then and me now is that I absolutely love food. I enjoy cooking. I love eating. The difference is, I now know when I have had my last bite and know when I am full. Food doesn't control me anymore.

As I lost the weight, food didn't call me—not exclusively because of my changing eating habits, but also because I no longer searched for strength, self-worth, and peace outside of myself.

And this is really about health, not weight loss. Pressing the pause button is always going to guide you to better decisions, whether it's about food selection, an activity, or a stressful relationship. You'll never go wrong when you take a breath and stop to ask yourself:

- *What is this doing to my body?*
- *How is this going to help me?*
- *Is this going to work with my body, or work against me?*

Design your life to support what you actually need and want— mentally, physically, and emotionally. The triggers do not go away; they are always there in the shadows. Use the tools you have learned here to call them out. Remind yourself, *these foods don't love me like I love me. I know what is best for me.*

This book is predominantly about transforming from within and helping you make the right choices to achieve your goals. I am someone who was overweight, overeating, and looked pregnant when I wasn't. When I was eating the food that my body was designed to eat and making better choices, I began to heal my life on a very deep level—emotionally, mentally, and spiritually.

I finally chose myself.

Starting today, you choose you.

CONCLUSION

How would it feel to be free of food obsession and feel at peace in your body?

You want to lose weight and keep it off, but weight loss is ultimately a side effect of a deeper healing and transformation. When you take something away, you have to put something in its place and build new habits with new tools, so that your new relationship with food is not based on compulsion and obsession.

Feeling desperate can be the springboard we need to change our lives.

If you follow these guidelines laid out in this book, your health will improve. And I do mean health in every sense of the word: physical, mental, and emotional. The side effect of your new commitment to total wellbeing will be weight loss.

But by the time the weight starts coming off, you'll already feel good about yourself. You will be the person you were always meant to be. You will feel good about yourself regardless of the weight you lose—yet lose it you will.

In this book, we have covered so much ground on the journey towards your wellbeing. I hope you take these important lessons with you as you move forward into your new life:

- Your obsession with food is not something you have to live with.
- Using food to solve your problems only leads to a vicious cycle of fear, eating, and regret—which in turn causes you to continue eating to try to break free. It will never work.
- So much of our unhappiness in life comes from unrealistic expectations, but acceptance of reality frees you to move forward.
- Pressing the pause button to respond rather than react to situations allows you to make better choices.
- The PEACE method can be used to change your reactions to responses when it comes to food.
- Practising gratitude is one of the simplest tools to adjust your perspective and move towards acceptance.
- Self-care isn't selfish: it is crucial for your own wellbeing and will provide you the stamina to care for others as well.
- Strengthening your connections to others helps foster a sense of belonging and reduces the isolation that accompanies overeating.
- You have the power to love yourself in the ways you may not have been loved as a child.
- Difficult feelings will rise and pass if you allow yourself to experience them. They do not need to be numbed with food.
- Carrying shame can negatively affect the way you see the

world, but you do not have to shoulder this burden. You are worthy.

- You do not need to take on more than you can handle in order to please others. *No* is a complete sentence.
- The food industry profits from your cravings, but you can embrace healthy eating habits with natural food that hasn't been tampered with at a factory.

Now you have a different way to deal with painful situations and emotions that are based on nurturing, love, and understanding. By using these tools, you can find a deep peace and healing that leads to turning to life, not food.

When you internalise these lessons and begin to act on them, you're not giving something up—quite the contrary. A wide world of choices will open up to you, and your newfound freedom allows you to do what you truly want to do instead of living in the shadows of shame.

By making healthy choices, we don't merely lose weight. We also grow as human beings. We become the best version of ourselves and have so much more joy when we live proactively and not reactively. Life is much more manageable when we pause, take control, and respond thoughtfully.

The best way that I know to make better choices is to apply the principles of awareness, acceptance, and action to *all* aspects of our lives, not just to our eating. We are so used to running on empty and letting life happen to us, and our reactions are often filtered through our shame as we move from one drama to the next. When we *pause*, our choices are revealed. When we put the focus back on ourselves and give ourselves the care and love that we deserve, we can flip the switch back to proactive mode. This is where we begin to truly *live*.

I know all about waking up in the morning, already feeling bloated from the night before, overeating again, and feeling terrible about it. I know the first thing you want to do is eat, immediately, just to be able to deal with those regretful feelings before you could even think about being healthy. And then the next minute, you're thinking, *Well, today was another failure—I can't start over midday. I've now got to wait until tomorrow, and then I'll be good.* Lather, rinse, repeat.

Waiting until tomorrow is our old way of thinking. *Today* is where we shall reside, because it's where all the good stuff happens.

It's time to give yourself a break and start treating yourself the way you would love to be treated by others. Practice self-love, self-kindness, self-understanding, and remember that failure is the fertiliser for success. Mistakes are meant to propel us forward, and *no one is perfect*, regardless of how they appear on social media.

Losing weight *is* an inside job. You have to learn to deal with uncomfortable feelings without turning to food—feel a full spectrum of emotions, find joy, and trust the process.

You may have been waiting for the knight in shining armour to come and rescue you—but you have been the hero of your story all along. It is your time to shine.

My mission is to help you take the next steps towards your weight loss goals. Visit **www.KatyLandis.co.uk/resources** for bonus material and resources to help you on your journey.

You don't have to do it alone.

ACKNOWLEDGEMENTS

I would like to thank everybody I have ever worked with as a coach. You have opened your hearts to me, and I am deeply grateful.

Special thanks to the amazing Beth Trach, without whose sharp mind and patience this book would not be possible.

Thanks to all the wonderful women who helped along the way: Bianca Pahl, Ami Hendrickson, and Jess Lagreca. And to my soul sister, Juliet, for her love and support.

I would like to thank my family—Nick, Josh, and Jake—who fill up my heart.

Lastly, I would like to thank Olly, my dog, for keeping my feet warm whilst I was writing.

ABOUT THE AUTHOR

KATY LANDIS is a motivational speaker and nutrition and mindset coach who focuses on the root cause of emotional eating. She has a passion for helping people break the cycle of destructive overeating, develop positive habits, and form healthy relationships with food. She is committed to empowering others to reach their weight loss goals, nourish both body and soul, and transform their lives. She and her family live in the UK.

.

Printed in Great Britain
by Amazon